Getting Started with Simulink

Get up and running with Simulink with this hands-on, easy-to-read guide

Luca Zamboni

BIRMINGHAM - MUMBAI

Getting Started with Simulink

First published: October 2013

Production Reference: 1181013

Published by Packt Publishing Ltd.
Livery Place
35 Livery Street
Birmingham B3 2PB, UK.

ISBN 978-1-78217-138-6

www.packtpub.com

Cover Image by Irene Sánchez Guillén (irene.s.guillen@gmail.com)

Credits

Author
Luca Zamboni

Reviewers
Robin T. Bye

Marco Caputano

Mohamed H. Zaher

Acquisition Editors
Edward Gordon

Kevin Colaco

Commissioning Editor
Poonam Jain

Technical Editors
Pramod Kumavat

Krutika Parab

Nadeem N. Bagban

Copy Editors
Dipti Kapadia

Gladson Monteiro

Sayanee Mukherjee

Kirti Pai

Project Coordinator
Sherin Padayatty

Proofreader
Sandra Hopper

Indexer
Monica Ajmera Mehta

Graphics
Yuvraj Mannari

Production Coordinator
Pooja Chiplunkar

Cover Work
Pooja Chiplunkar

About the Author

Luca Zamboni, born in Ivrea, Italy, obtained his Bachelor's and Master's degrees in Electronics Engineering from the Polytechnic of Turin. He worked as a network systems administrator for some years before becoming a consultant for the automotive industry. Now he works in FIAT's research center.

About the Reviewers

Robin T. Bye, got his Bachelor's, Master's, and PhD degrees, all in Electrical Engineering, from the University of New South Wales, Sydney, Australia. He has been working at the Aalesund University College (AAUC) in Norway since 2008 and is now an associate professor in automation engineering. Apart from teaching automation and computer engineering classes for cybernetics, microcontrollers, and intelligent systems, he also supervises PhD and bachelor students on their theses' topics. His main research interests belong to areas such as computational modeling and simulation of human movements, bio-inspired robotics and automation, and dynamic resource allocation.

Marco Caputano was born in Southern Italy in 1980. He has obtained an M.Sc. in Control Engineering from the University of Napoli Federico II in Italy. His final dissertation was on nuclear plasma modeling in the framework of nuclear fusion research. He broadened his academic education with a Masters in Mechatronic Systems Design obtained from the Engineering Polytechnic of Milano, Italy. His former work activities include modeling and numerical simulations for nuclear fusion research (CREATE consortium, Napoli, Italy), and in the field of aeronautical engineering (SAFRAN group, Paris, France). Currently, he works as a Mechatronics Engineer for ASML in the Netherlands.

Mohamed H. Zaher is from Egypt; he is a Mechatronics and Controls Engineer. He received both his Bachelor's and Master's degrees in Mechanical Engineering with System Dynamics and Mechatronics Focus from Cairo University in Egypt and his Ph.D from University of Illinois at Chicago. Mohamed taught mechanical engineering curriculum at both universities including the use of software tools such as MATLAB and Simulink. He also worked on contract at Caterpillar, Case New Holland, and Servo Tech Inc., where he worked with several professional tools on several developmental projects.

www.PacktPub.com

Support files, eBooks, discount offers and more

You might want to visit www.PacktPub.com for support files and downloads related to your book.

Did you know that Packt offers eBook versions of every book published, with PDF and ePub files available? You can upgrade to the eBook version at www.PacktPub.com and as a print book customer, you are entitled to a discount on the eBook copy. Get in touch with us at service@packtpub.com for more details.

At www.PacktPub.com, you can also read a collection of free technical articles, sign up for a range of free newsletters and receive exclusive discounts and offers on Packt books and eBooks.

http://PacktLib.PacktPub.com

Do you need instant solutions to your IT questions? PacktLib is Packt's online digital book library. Here, you can access, read, and search across Packt's entire library of books.

Why Subscribe?

- Fully searchable across every book published by Packt
- Copy and paste, print, and bookmark content
- On demand and accessible via web browser

Free Access for Packt account holders

If you have an account with Packt at www.PacktPub.com, you can use this to access PacktLib today and view nine entirely free books. Simply use your login credentials for immediate access.

Instant Updates on New Packt Books

Get notified! Find out when new books are published by following @PacktEnterprise on Twitter, or the *Packt Enterprise* Facebook page.

Table of Contents

Preface

This book will give you a complete understanding of the Simulink software. You will learn by example, going through the three main phases of Simulink development—modeling, simulating, and interfacing with the external world while developing a cruise controller for a real car.

While reading this book, you'll be given a clear, no-frills explanation of the main components of Simulink and how to use them in order to achieve the desired result. After having read this book, you will be able to develop, test, and deploy your models without any difficulty.

What this book covers

Chapter 1, Simulink Facts, deals with the problems that arise while developing the software for the biggest manufacturing industries and how Simulink can cut down the total development time, from specifications to final implementation. You will understand where Simulink really shines and where it isn't worth the hassle.

Chapter 2, Creating a Model, deals with developing a very simple cruise controller model in order to get started quickly with Simulink and the MATLAB environment. Then you will be guided through the Simulink implementation of a real-world car to use with the previously developed cruise controller, thus introducing the usage of more complex blocks. You will understand how a model is developed and where to look for the appropriate blocks.

Chapter 3, Simulating a Model, deals with presenting the theory behind simulation: solvers, simulation times, and how to choose them. You will then simulate the models you already developed, learning what are the available sources and sinks blocks and when to use them in order to discover failures in your models and change some of the parameters you defined.

Chapter 4, Using the Model, guides you through the most powerful feature of Simulink — the ability to create your own blocks, also known as S-function development — after having learned how to develop and simulate a model. You will create a simple S-function that enables your cruise controller to drive an external application and receive feedback from it.

What you need for this book

You should have a working MATLAB installation with the Simulink package. While this book has been written using the 8.1 (R2013a) release, you aren't required to use this exact version, as there are only minor differences between one release and another; the basic workflow remains the same. But you'll need at least the 8.1 release to be able to run the provided code.

In order to develop and test S-functions, you should have a compiler supported by your MATLAB release.

Who this book is for

This book is aimed at undergraduate students, researchers, and engineers who need to have a quick and complete understanding of how Simulink works, including some of its most advanced features.

The reader should have basic knowledge of physics and C programming.

Conventions

In this book, you will find a number of styles of text that distinguish between different kinds of information. Here are some examples of these styles, and an explanation of their meaning.

Code words in text, database table names, folder names, filenames, file extensions, pathnames, dummy URLs, user input, and Twitter handles are shown as follows: While, to a certain degree, it is possible to spot the differences when saving models with the `.mdl` format.

A block of code is set as follows:

```
    int main()
{
    int u1, u2, y1;
    printf(""Enter two numbers\n"");
    scanf(""%d%d"", &u1, &u2);
    y1 = mul(u1, u2);
    printf(""Here''s your result,
       the operation done is a shining ''x''!\n%d\n"", y1);
         return EXIT_SUCCESS;
}
```

Any command-line input or output is written as follows:

```
new_string = 'hello world!';
new_number = 0.01;
```

New terms and **important words** are shown in bold. Words that you see on the screen, in menus or dialog boxes for example, appear in the text like this: "From the MATLAB main window, click on the **New** button and select the **Simulink Model** option".

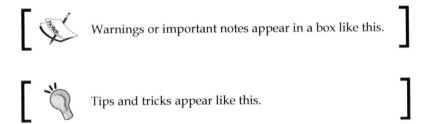

Warnings or important notes appear in a box like this.

Tips and tricks appear like this.

Reader feedback

Feedback from our readers is always welcome. Let us know what you think about this book—what you liked or may have disliked. Reader feedback is important for us to develop titles that you really get the most out of.

To send us general feedback, simply send an e-mail to feedback@packtpub.com, and mention the book title via the subject of your message.

If there is a topic that you have expertise in and you are interested in either writing or contributing to a book, see our author guide on www.packtpub.com/authors.

Customer support

Now that you are the proud owner of a Packt book, we have a number of things to help you to get the most from your purchase.

Downloading the example code

You can download the example code files for all Packt books you have purchased from your account at `http://www.packtpub.com`. If you purchased this book elsewhere, you can visit `http://www.packtpub.com/support` and register to have the files e-mailed directly to you.

Errata

Although we have taken every care to ensure the accuracy of our content, mistakes do happen. If you find a mistake in one of our books—maybe a mistake in the text or the code—we would be grateful if you would report this to us. By doing so, you can save other readers from frustration and help us improve subsequent versions of this book. If you find any errata, please report them by visiting `http://www.packtpub.com/submit-errata`, selecting your book, clicking on the **errata submission form** link, and entering the details of your errata. Once your errata are verified, your submission will be accepted and the errata will be uploaded on our website, or added to any list of existing errata, under the Errata section of that title. Any existing errata can be viewed by selecting your title from `http://www.packtpub.com/support`.

Piracy

Piracy of copyright material on the Internet is an ongoing problem across all media. At Packt, we take the protection of our copyright and licenses very seriously. If you come across any illegal copies of our works, in any form, on the Internet, please provide us with the location address or website name immediately so that we can pursue a remedy.

Please contact us at `copyright@packtpub.com` with a link to the suspected pirated material.

We appreciate your help in protecting our authors, and our ability to bring you valuable content.

Questions

You can contact us at `questions@packtpub.com` if you are having a problem with any aspect of the book, and we will do our best to address it.

1
Simulink Facts

In this chapter, we'll explain what Simulink is, and why it has been so widely adopted in the academic and the industrial world.

After reading this chapter, you'll have learned about the limits of the usual C software development cycle, and how Simulink helps to address these limits.

What is Simulink?

Simulink is best described as a graphical programming tool. Let's elaborate a little on these two words.

Programming

Since the start of the digital era, telling a computer what to do has been a huge problem. Humans communicate through a set of conventions — languages — with very elaborate rules, definitions, and exceptions. New languages aren't easily born in the human world. But what about computers? They operate by means of a stream of zeros and ones, using Boolean logic; that's the binary system. The computer language is nowhere as complex as the human language, but how fast are computers at solving logical problems! The difficulty is in telling the computer how to solve a given problem, and this is the art of programming.

Nowadays there are so many programming languages that knowing at least one is as common as knowing more than one human language. Those lucky ones who do are called programmers. They're able to write the instructions that a computer has to execute (and the computer understands them — well, most of the time).

Writing and debugging a complex, real-time, safety-critical application is not a trivial task, and in big automotive/aerospace industries, a misbehaving software is definitely not an option. As an example, the 327.6 million dollars NASA Mars Climate Orbiter space probe disintegrated before landing because the ground control software used the imperial metric system instead of the international one. It sounds funny, but imagine what would happen if your car maker made such a mistake in the brake control software?

The problem with using the venerable, almighty C—still the language of choice for embedded systems—is that it isn't easy to scale up the system complexity. It's interesting to note that while the system gets bigger, the deadlines get narrower. The good old tools (code editors, compilers, and debuggers) aren't effective anymore to keep the whole development time constant while raising the software requirements.

Graphical

This is the next step.

Imagine an Italian guy in Moscow willing to buy a bottle of water. Chances are that he doesn't know one word of Russian, nor the Russian shop owner knows more than two words of Italian (bella and ciao).

Our Italian guy would likely point at a bottle of water with his finger and mimic the act of drinking. The Russian shop owner would smile to acknowledge the request, and then use his fingers (or pencil and paper) to communicate the price to pay.

So what? We had visual communication. The simplest of all languages are the visual ones.

When a programmer tries to explain to his manager how a code works, he usually starts drawing blocks on a piece of paper—something like the following oversimplified example:

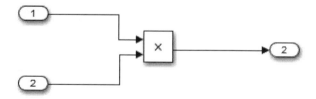

It isn't hard to understand that the logic flows from left to right (because of the arrows), and that two inputs will be multiplied together to obtain the output. With nothing more than a simple glance, you've understood what the computer has been programmed to do.

Let's compare it with a warning-free, standards-compliant C code:

```c
#include <stdio.h>
#include <stdlib.h>

int mul(int, int);

int main()
{
    int u1, u2, y1;
    printf("Enter two numbers\n");
    scanf("%d%d", &u1, &u2);
    y1 = mul(u1, u2);
    printf("Here's your result,
  the operation done is a shining 'x'!\n%d\n", y1);
    return EXIT_SUCCESS;
}

int mul(int input1, int input2)
{
    return input1*input2;
}
```

Now chances are one of the following:

* You know C, and you understood what the code does after reading through it
* You don't know C, but you know other programming languages; maybe you haven't understood every line, but you are still able to figure out what the program does
* You don't know any programming language; you're almost clueless and you understand what's going on only because you've seen the figure first

Either way, a visual representation of the code is much easier to understand and maintain.

Now imagine a long (several hundred lines), complex (tens of source files) code, poorly commented, highly optimized for a certain processor architecture, edited by several people without a strict style policy — the classic spaghetti code that many programmers are faced with in their job. They'll spend a huge amount of time understanding what the code does, no matter how skilled they are. Explaining that code to a colleague who doesn't know programming is out of the question.

That's where visual programming comes the rescue. A graphical programming tool can save countless hours of work in a job where explaining the code is as important as a code without bugs, or where a bug can have disastrous (safety-critical) effects.

Simulink is such a tool.

Problems solved by Simulink

Simulink is a true life saver in large companies manufacturing safety-critical products, or where the software development is usually split into three different phases:

- **Specification phase**: The algorithm is planned or updated by the specification team and a new specification is released
- **Development phase**: The algorithm is implemented by the development team and a software release is made
- **Testing phase**: The software undergoes an extensive testing phase both on simulated and on real hardware; only when the test results are positive, the testing team states that the software is ready for production

Software specification

In every software project where safety is an issue, the software development starts only when a stable specification has been released.

Specifications are usually written as text documents where each sentence describes an atomic requirement and must be highly detailed.

The problem with specifications as text documents is that there isn't any way of verifying the correctness of the specified logic until the development phase or even the testing phase.

Every time that the specification is found to be incorrect or incomplete, the specification team must be notified and must make a new release. So the development team has to develop the new release, likewise the testing team will have to test the new software.

A specification error is one of the worst things that can happen in a big manufacturing company, often leading to production delays, while underspecified software can lead to unwanted behavior.

Simulink can be used to achieve the goal of writing correct and complete specifications, without losing anything in readability. Let's consider the following atomic requirement:

REQUIREMENT # 101:

If **InputSignal** *is greater than* **0**, *the* **InputSignalFlag** *variable must be set.*

The corresponding Simulink block would be as follows:

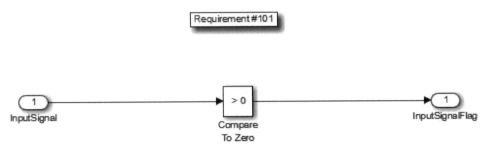

What's the real deal? It is that you can test the requirement before it's released. With Simulink, it's easy to generate input signals and register the output as shown in the following diagram:

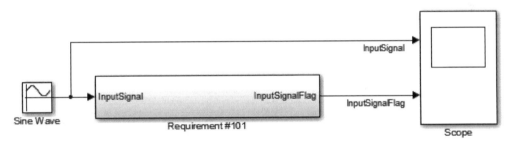

When viewing the display on **Scope**, the result will look like the following diagram:

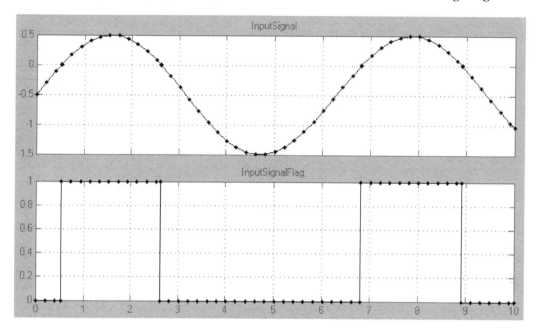

But wait! Let's examine the textual requirement; it says that the flag must be set. It's unclear (not specified) whether the **InputSignalFlag** variable should be reset when **InputSignal** becomes 0 or less than 0.

But the difference is very clear in a specification done with Simulink. The following is the block diagram that describes the requirement with the **InputSignalFlag** variable remaining set until the end of the execution cycle:

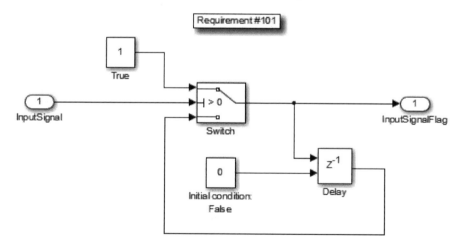

We can see that the simulation result is very different from the previous one, as seen in the following diagram:

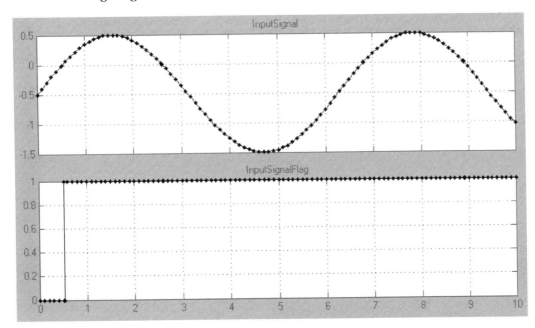

With textual requirements, there's always a gray area due to the fact that human languages, despite their richness (or because of it), have problems in describing a Boolean logic. And it's extremely difficult, if not impossible, to test the requirement before the release.

With Simulink models as requirements, there is no room for doubt. The requirement is complete and easily understandable by nonprogrammers, and a preliminary test can be made with little to zero effort by the very same team that wrote it.

Software development

The development team has the responsibility of maintaining and updating the software for a certain project or series of projects. The usual work flow for the embedded C developer of an automotive industry is shown in the following diagram:

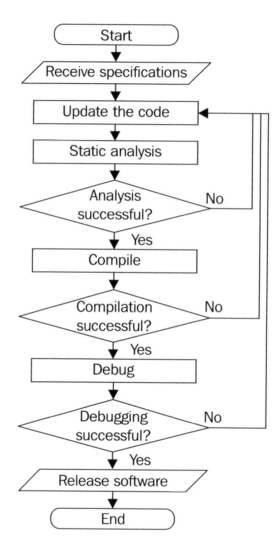

The first problem developers are faced with is the code itself. A well-commented code with strict coding-style guidelines will be easily understandable and maintainable, but sadly, that's not the common situation. Code maintainability is a major issue almost everywhere, strictly dependent on code readability.

The second problem is the formal code-correctness checking. This means doing a static code analysis to check compliance with one or more sets of formal rules (for example, the MISRA-C rule set).

The third and the most important problem is code debugging. This is done by running the code to do an early testing (for example, with `valgrind`) and applying well-known input patterns to detect and correct the blocking bugs.

Simulink helps the pressed developer solve these problems in the following ways:.

- **Code readability**: Being a graphical development tool, developers have an intuitive way of dividing the code into multilayered virtual blocks. The topmost layers give a representation of the functionality subsets implemented, while the lower layers contain the code primitives (logical and mathematical operators, memories, state machines, and so on).

- **Static code analysis**: By using Simulink with code generation software (Simulink coder—formerly Real-Time Workshop—and DSpace TargetLink are the most popular), it is possible to produce error-free embedded C code. They guarantee that the produced code offers the same functionality described in the model.

- **Code debugging**: During model development, Simulink offers the option to do an early testing; the developer can apply an input pattern to a well-known problematic algorithm and visualize the simulation result, inspect every signal, do a step-by-step debug, and stop the simulation on selected events on the same model used for code generation.

By using Simulink, the development team can apply the required updates in a shorter time and use the remaining time to perform a quick preliminary testing of the code.

Static code analysis becomes almost irrelevant since coding rules and conventions are enforced by the code generation software.

Finally, with the autogenerated code being free of syntax errors, the compilation phase is usually straightforward. This greatly helps the programmer who is not familiar with the C syntax.

Software testing

The released code needs an extensive testing phase before being put into production. The testing team's objective is to confirm that the software is compliant with the specifications.

This usually involves breaking the specifications into atomic requirements and having one or more test cases for each requirement (the so-called functional testing), or defining what should never happen and automatically apply every possible combination of inputs to the software component (a subset of destructive testing).

By using Simulink models, the testing team can easily perform automatic **model-in-the-loop** (**MIL**) testing on their computers; the logical correctness is demonstrated by applying inputs to the Simulink models and comparing the outputs to the expected behavior. MIL testing easily spots failures in a very short time and generates a detailed test report, even pinpointing the model block where the problem resides. MATLAB already has everything needed to perform an MIL test, while automated tests can be coded using the MATLAB scripting language.

Once the MIL testing is successful, the **software-in-the-loop** (**SIL**) testing is performed by running the autogenerated code on standard computers. It is usually aimed at finding discrepancies between the model and the code behaviors, and it requires another software monitoring the process's I/O or the inclusion of debug headers into the tested code, or a mixture of both.

The next testing step is the **processor-in-the-loop(PIL)** testing, where the software is programmed into the target processor and debugged via an external high-speed bus connected to a standard computer, such as a JTAG connection. Of course this requires having the target processor available on a board with a testing connection.

The last step is to perform **hardware-in-the-loop** (**HIL**) testing, which is running the software on the target hardware connected to a real-time system. It requires a custom test bench to be purchased or made internally, and some test steps have to be executed manually.

The biggest advantage of MIL testing is to reduce the number of times SIL, PIL, and HIL tests are performed. This is because most of the problems are caught during the fast, nonexpensive MIL tests, thereby reducing the overall time spent to generate, build, and validate the produced code.

Simulink drawbacks

Simulink isn't the way to go for small projects with a low budget: a MATLAB license is rather expensive: like the additional packages that may be required for testing on dedicated hardware. It is suited for big projects with a large number of developers working on them. A skilled C developer can write code for simple to trivial projects in a much shorter time than by dragging blocks in Simulink.

MATLAB and Simulink are targeted specifically to engineering and scientific applications; they aren't general-purpose-programming tools. It's difficult, though not impossible, to develop desktop applications or web services using Simulink.

Finally, it's hard to track model changes with software versioning and revision control systems (such as CVS, SVN, Git, Bazaar, or Mercurial). While, to a certain degree, it is possible to spot the differences when saving models with the .mdl format (because it's a structured text file), this has become difficult with the .slx format (a zipped archive with more information on the model). To see and highlight the differences between two versions of the same model, separate software has to be purchased.

Where Simulink excels

There are two main use cases for Simulink.

The first one is in the academic research world where Simulink is used to simulate multidomain dynamic systems. Typically, Simulink is used in a continuous-time environment with variable step-size implicit solvers; the main scope of the simulation is to reproduce the behavior of a real system in order to predict the answer to the applied stimuli.

The second one is in the automotive, aerospace, avionics, and the defense industry where Simulink is used to build models for real-time, safety-critical, embedded targets with many people involved in the specification, development, and testing phases. The main scope of the simulation is to find and correct bugs in order to produce (through the appropriate code-generation software) a final C code to compile in the target processor. The simulation solver used in this environment is the fixed-size step explicit one, and the model doesn't contain any continuous states.

Summary

In this chapter we learned what benefits Simulink brings in and where Simulink has become a de-facto standard and why. We explained how the software development process is simplified using Simulink and cases where Simulink is not the right solution. After reading this chapter, you should be able to decide whether Simulink can be used for your projects.

In the following chapters, we'll take a learn-by-doing approach where we'll go through the whole software development process while developing and testing a cruise controller model for a real-world car.

2
Creating a Model

In this chapter, we'll learn how to build a Simulink model and run the first simulations.

We'll start with a short description of the MATLAB environment features that we need to know in order to start developing a Simulink model.

Then we'll build a simple model to introduce the basics of Simulink development; we'll learn what the Library Browser is and how to place blocks into the Model Editor.

Finally, we'll develop a more complex model implementing a not-so-simple nonlinear system. There will be a small part of theory detailing the physic equations describing the system before the implementation.

The MATLAB environment

Simulink is not a standalone tool, but lies on MATLAB's shoulders; it's almost impossible to use Simulink without keeping an eye on MATLAB's main window, not to mention that you need to start MATLAB before even opening a model.

Simulink inherits from MATLAB the current working folder, the workspace, and the path and uses MATLAB's **Command Window** to report errors, warnings, and notes.

The first time you open MATLAB, you should see the default main window view with the following sections:

- The **Workspace** panel and the **Command History** panel on the right
- The **Command Window** panel in the middle
- The **Current Folder** panel with the folder contents on the left.
- The current path is displayed above the three

An example is shown in the following screenshot:

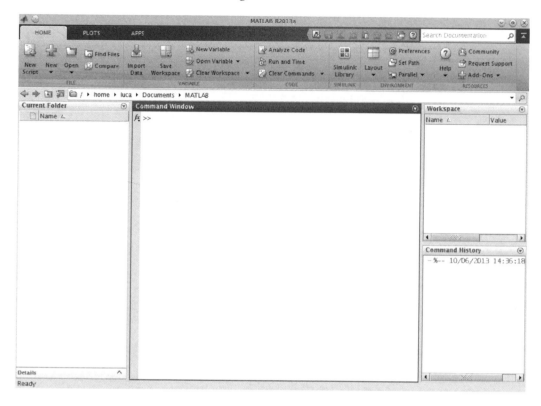

Command Window – how MATLAB talks to us

The **Command Window** panel is the place where Simulink will report most of the errors, warnings, and information—always keep an eye on it while debugging a model!

The **Command Window** panel also allows us to declare new variables that will be stored into the workspace. In short, the **Command Window** panel works very much like any interactive OS terminal shell, accepting commands written in the MATLAB language.

The MATLAB interface being written in Java, you can even create and use Java objects!

Try entering these two commands and see what happens:

```
new_string = 'hello world!';
new_number = 0.01;
```

The newly created variables have appeared in the **Workspace** panel and are ready to use.

It's worth noting that every command executed is stored in the **Command History** panel too; if you need to re-execute a command you entered earlier, simply drag-and-drop it into the **Command Window** panel.

 The **Command Window** panel supports autocompletion; you only need to type the first characters of a command or variable name and hit the *Tab* key – MATLAB will show the matching labels.

The workspace – our treasury chest

The workspace holds the variables we create in the session, allowing you to edit and delete them through the **Workspace** panel.

Simulink is able to see the variables in the workspace and use them in the model. From Simulink's perspective, they belong to the base workspace.

Keep in mind that the workspace resides in volatile memory and is not persistent; as soon as MATLAB is closed, the workspace is lost.

To save the workspace into a MATLAB file (with the `.mat` extension), click on the **Save Workspace** button in the **HOME** tab. MATLAB will ask you where you wish to store it, with the working folder as the default choice.

The working folder – where MATLAB saves our work

The working folder (called **Current Folder** in MATLAB's main window) is the folder that is currently open in MATLAB and all the files contained here are visible to MATLAB and Simulink. The exact path of the working folder is shown in the address bar right above the **Command Window**, the **Workspace**, and the **Current Folder** panels.

To execute a file, you can simply drag-and-drop the file from the **Current Folder** panel to the **Command Window** panel. This works with all MATLAB and Simulink files.

The path – where MATLAB finds the tools

The path variable is the list of folders where MATLAB will look for libraries at startup (this is very similar to how the $PATH variable is used in most operating systems). If you need to use a Simulink blockset (a library of ready-to-use blocks), you must place it into a folder listed in your MATLAB's path.

You can easily view and edit MATLAB's path by clicking on the **Set Path** icon in the **HOME** tab. A new window will appear, listing every folder present in MATLAB's path and giving you the option to add other folders and change the order in which they appear.

The display order is important; if a file with the same name is present in two or more folders listed in the path variable, MATLAB will use the one found in the folder nearest to the top of the search path.

The exact file where the path variable is stored is the pathdef.m script, located in your MATLAB install folder (usually $MATLABROOT/toolbox/local).

If you don't remember where you've installed MATLAB, just enter matlabroot in the **Command Window**.

A great thing to have in the path is a customized startup script; if you need to execute a set of commands every time MATLAB starts, put them in a startup.m script and save the script in one of the folders belonging to MATLAB's path.

If you've added too many folders to the path and something is going wrong, you can restore the default path with the restoredefaultpath command.

This is all you need to know about the MATLAB environment.

Remember that Simulink is reading everything from MATLAB and you will save yourself a lot of trouble.

The Simulink interface

From the MATLAB main window, click on the **New** button and select the **Simulink Model** option.

A blank Simulink window will appear, showing an empty model named **untitled**. This window is made up of the following sections:

- The title bar with the name of the opened system (**untitled**).
- The menu bar immediately below the title bar.
- The toolbar below the menu bar with the default tools (the **Library Browser** and **Model Explorer** are the tools most used).
- The **Model Browser** panel on the left displaying the model's hierarchical tree (it can be hidden with the « button at the bottom right of this panel).
- The model editor panel on the right of the **Model Browser** panel is the most useful panel. If you like a clutter-free edit window, you can hide all the other panels through the **View** menu (I suggest that you leave the status bar though).
- The status bar on the bottom reporting the name and the current status of the underlying simulation solver (more on this later).

The most useful shortcuts and gestures are as follows:

- Zooming in/out can be done with the mouse's scroll wheel
- If you wish the scroll wheel to retain its usual behavior (just scrolling up and down), then navigate to **File | Simulink Preferences | Editor defaults** and clear the **Scroll wheel controls zooming** checkbox; zooming is still possible by pressing the *Ctrl* key while scrolling
- Tapping the Space bar key will make the model view (or the selected block view) fit the window size
- Pressing *Alt + 1* resets the default zoom (it's a lifesaver!)
- Pressing and keeping the mouse wheel pressed will allow you to drag the model in the direction of the mouse, an operation known as panning
- If you don't have the scroll wheel, you can achieve panning by keeping the Space bar key and the left mouse button pressed

We'll talk extensively about the Library Browser in the following paragraphs. Now it's time to start modeling!

Our first model – a cruise controller

There aren't many things in the world funnier than a sporty car. That's a fact.

Let's imagine we want to develop a simple cruise control system for such a car. This system will perform the following tasks:

- Read the target vehicle speed [km/h]
- Read the current vehicle speed [km/h]
- Command the throttle with the gas pedal [from 0 (not pressed) to 1 (fully pressed)]

This system will behave like a driver that keeps the car going straight using only the gas pedal to match the desired speed.

Let's get started!

Step 1 – create and save the model

After pointing MATLAB to your preferred working folder (for example, a folder called `1386EN_02` located in your home folder) and opening a new model, click on the **Save** button, or use the **Save** option under the **File** menu, or the *Ctrl + S* keyboard shortcut, and give it the name `cruise_control.slx`.

You'll notice that there are two file formats available. They are explained as follows:

- The `.mdl` extension was the format used by Simulink versions prior to MATLAB R2012a (a structured text file)
- The `.slx` extension is the format used by newer Simulink versions, introduced in MATLAB R2012a (a compressed group of files)

The first format is the most widely used, but be aware that every model depends on the Simulink version used to create it; those developed with newer releases are unreadable by older releases, while newer releases can upgrade old models.

The saved model will now be visible in our working folder. If you close Simulink, you can re-open the model at a later time by dragging it to the MATLAB's **Command Window**.

Step 2 – do comment the code!

It's always a good idea to explain what a system does. In the C programming language, you use the comment section (/* ... */) to explain a function; in Simulink, you insert a note by clicking on the **Annotation** tool icon (to the left of our **cruise_control** editor panel) or double-clicking on the white area of the model editor.

Like comments explaining functions in C, it's a good practice to insert a note at the top of the model view explaining what it does. Let's insert this note:

```
This model simulates a cruise control system.

The purpose is to make a car going at a desired

speed using the throttle.
```

By right-clicking on the note, you can set the alignment (default: centered) and draw an annotation border, to make it more eye-catching:

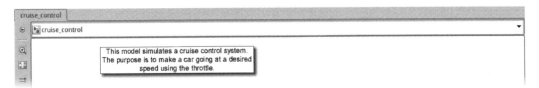

Step 3 – open Simulink Library Browser

Let's start inserting some blocks from the Simulink library. We need to open the **Simulink Library Browser** by pressing the **Library Browser** button, or using the **View | Library Browser** menu, or using the *Ctrl + Shift + L* keyboard shortcut.

A new window with two panels will appear: the left panel lists all the available libraries, each one holding one or more subsets, while the right panel shows all the blocks belonging to the selected library. Block libraries are also called blocksets.

By double-clicking on a block, a new window appears with a brief block description and the parameters that the block can accept. To get detailed information about the block and how to use it, click on the **Help** button and the documentation center will be opened with the page describing the selected block's meaning and usage.

Navigating in the **Simulink Library Browser** is fairly straightforward; most of the time we'll be using blocks from the **Simulink** blockset (installed with the Simulink software).

Both the **Simulink Library Browser** and the documentation center have a search input field located above the main window content, allowing you to get the block itself and its documentation by entering the block name (or part of it).

Step 4 – add blocks to the model from Library Browser

The first blocks we need are input and output ports. Input ports (also called inports) are available in the **Simulink | Sources** blockset and are labeled **In1**:

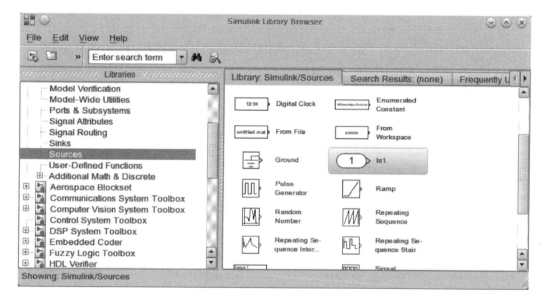

Similarly, output ports are available in the **Simulink | Sinks** blockset and are labeled **Out1**.

These blocks can be placed in the model by:

- Dragging and dropping from the Library Browser to the model window, or
- Copying and pasting (*Ctrl + C, Ctrl + V*) to the model window, or
- Right-clicking and selecting the option **Add to cruise_control**, or
- Using the keyboard shortcut *Ctrl + I* (insert)

Let's place one input port and one output port in the model using your preferred method.

Notice that the window title has changed and now bears an asterisk (**cruise_control ***). This means that the model has been edited since the last save. Save the model and the asterisk will go away.

Of course, opening the **Simulink Library Browser** each time you need to place a block is a tedious task and slows down development time. If a block offering the same functionality is already present in the model, you can just copy and paste it, or drag it while keeping the right mouse button pressed; a new copy will be made.

Let's add another input port by moving the mouse arrow on the previous port, and while keeping the right mouse button pressed drag it to some other position and then release the button; a small menu will appear asking you if you intend to **Paste** or **Duplicate** the port:

- **Paste**: This option creates a new port, adding a new input signal to the subsystem.
- **Duplicate**: This option will not add a new input signal; the new port will be equal to the copied one and the signal will be the same. It's useful only to avoid a connecting line.

Notice that while dragging a block, Simulink suggests the alignment with other ports, which helps in keeping the project well-structured.

If we don't spend a little time in trying to keep the system view well organized, we'll end up with a garbled system that very much resembles the dreaded "spaghetti code" that we should avoid.

A set of rules has been defined by the MathWorks Automotive Advisory Board with the automotive industry in mind. Embedded developers with code generation in mind should stick to it as closely as possible. The ruleset is available at `http://www.mathworks.com/automotive/standards/maab.html`.

Step 5 – rename the blocks

Note that each block must have a unique name in the current subsystem. Try to rename the **In2** port to **In1** by double-clicking on its name; Simulink will issue an error window saying that the name already exists.

Since the labels **In1** and **In2** don't make a lot of sense, we'll rename them to our inputs: the **Vehicle speed** and the **Target speed**. The same goes for our output: the **Throttle**.

> A good practice is to put the measurement unit in the name too; it helps to avoid conversion errors (even the best can make such errors — the NASA did!).

Now we should have something similar to the following screenshot:

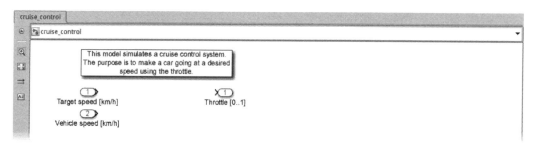

Step 6 – implement the algorithm

The simplest yet most effective cruise control algorithm is a PI (Proportional-Integral) controller. This algorithm can be summarized in the following four steps:

1. Calculate the error **e(t)**, that is, the difference between the target speed and the vehicle speed.
2. Apply a correction factor to the error K_p.
3. Apply a correction factor to the integral of the error, K_i.
4. Sum both the proportional and the integral components and obtain the control signal **u(t)**.

The mathematical formula of a PI controller is as follows:

$$u(t) = K_p e(t) + K_i \int_0^t e(\tau) d\tau$$

Of course, we can't push the gas pedal beyond its physical limits; the throttle control signal needs to be clamped, the lower limit being 0 (throttle closed) and the higher limit being 1 (throttle fully open).

By looking at the formula, it's easy to guess that we need to find the following blocks in the **Simulink Library Browser**:

- One **Subtract** block (from **Simulink | Math Operations**) in order to calculate the error

- Two **Constant** blocks (from **Simulink | Sources**) for Kp and Ki, and two **Product** blocks (from **Simulink | Math Operations**)

- One **Integrator** block (from **Simulink | Continuous**) used to hold the error integral

- One **Add** block (from **Simulink | Math Operations**)

- One **Saturation** block (from **Simulink | Discontinuities**) to clamp the output throttle

> The **Integrator** block (and almost every other block in the **Continuous** blockset) is represented with the corresponding transfer function H(s) = Y(s)/U(s) in the Laplace domain. More information can be obtained by clicking on the **Help** button in the block parameters window.
>
> You don't need to know about Laplace transforms in order to understand this book; just remember that the **1/s** block is an integrator.

Place the blocks in the order suggested by the algorithm (refer to the following screenshot) and open every block to understand its options. Don't forget to:

- Check the **Subtract** block operands: the **Target speed** has to be connected to the positive port and the **Vehicle speed** to the negative port; thus the block parameter should be +–

- Edit the **Saturation** block limits by double-clicking on it; a window opens; in that window, set the value of **Upper limit:** as 1 and the value of **Lower limit:** as 0

Optionally, resize the blocks (by dragging the little handles that appear on the selected block's border), hide the math blocks' names (by right-clicking on the blocks and opening the **Format** submenu), and rename the constant blocks to **Ki** and **Kp**.

To connect two blocks, it's sufficient to drag the little arrow from the source block to the endpoint at the destination block with the mouse.

> To quickly connect two blocks, select the source block, then press and hold the *Ctrl* key, and click on the destination block. This works with multiple blocks too.

We should end up with a model similar to the one shown in the following screenshot:

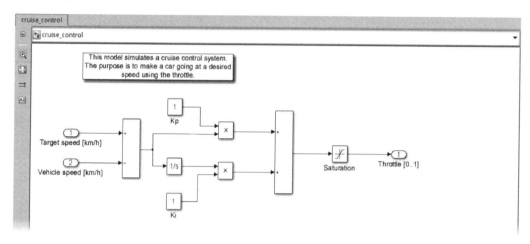

Step 7 – nest the logic into subsystems

Subsystems are a very convenient way to group together the blocks that implement a specific functionality.

In order to make a clear distinction between the PI controller components, we can select the elements to group together and right-click the selection to open the contextual menu and create a subsystem (or use the *Ctrl + G* keyboard shortcut). The operation is shown in the following screenshot:

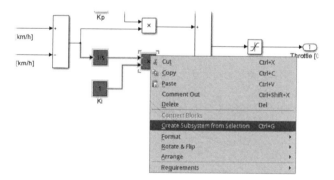

We'll create two subsystems: one for the proportional component and one for the integral component. Since they are of a small default size and have the default port names of **In1** and **Out1**, we should resize and rename them, then open them (with a double click) and rename their ports.

We should obtain the model shown in the following screenshot:

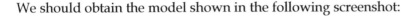

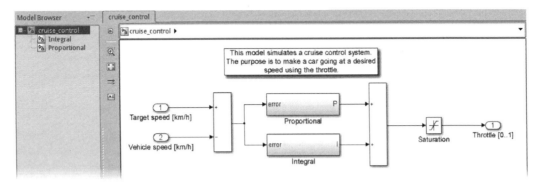

Notice the change in the **Model Browser** panel on the left; you can now navigate in your system hierarchy by clicking on the subsystems' names. The **cruise_control** block is called the root subsystem.

Let's continue organizing the model into subsystems by selecting all the PI controller components (everything except the ports and the **Saturation** block) and making a subsystem. Again, we need to edit the new subsystem's port names.

We should see the clean, ordered, neat-looking, self-explanatory system shown in the following screenshot:

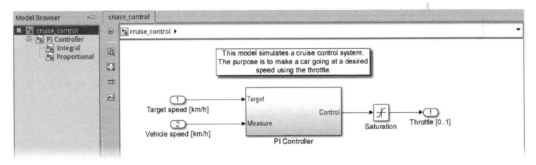

The final step—the root subsystem should contain absolutely no logic, only root-level blocks implementing a complete functionality, sharing little to no signals. We still have the **Saturation** block left out.

So we'll select everything (literally—ports included) and create the cruise control root subsystem as shown in the following screenshot:

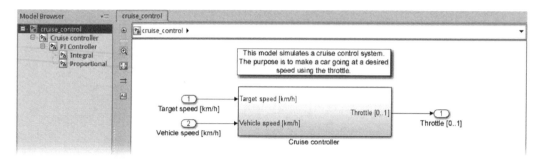

This time we didn't have to rename the ports; since we included them inside the selection, Simulink kept their names and created new copies outside the newly created subsystem.

Step 8 – declare workspace variables

There's a problem with the cruise controller; we've left the PI calibration constants inside the block, and we can't calibrate them without doing some simulations.

This means that either we dig into the model hierarchy down to the Integral and Proportional blocks every time we need to change their values, or we pull them out to the root level.

Both of these methods are viable with a simple system like the one we've just modeled. But as soon as the model complexity grows, you'll have problems either in knowing where the constants are or in having a clean, understandable system layout.

But there is a clean and effective solution. Since Simulink can read MATLAB's variables, it's easy to define the K_p and K_i constants in the MATLAB workspace and use their labels in the Constant blocks.

So we define them by entering these commands in MATLAB's **Command Window**:

```
Kp = 1;
Ki = 1;
```

Then we'll navigate to the constant blocks, double-click each one of them and edit the **Constant Value** field in their respective **Source Block Parameters** window with the previously defined variables Kp and Ki.

The block parameters window for Kp will look like the following screenshot:

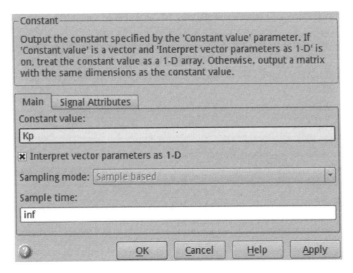

Done! Now we can edit Kp and Ki directly from the MATLAB's **Command Window!**

Let's save the workspace alongside the model, (that is, at the same location where cruise_control.slx is saved) calling it cruise_control.mat (click on the **Save Workspace** button in MATLAB's main window.).

To avoid loading it every time we open the model, we can use the PreLoadFcn model callback. Navigate to the root subsystem, right-click on the white space, and choose the **Model Properties** item from the contextual menu. A new window will open; click on the **Callbacks** tab and select the **PreLoadFcn** item from the list. Inside the textbox, we'll type the MATLAB command that will perform the workspace loading: load('cruise_control.mat').

To confirm that we didn't make trivial mistakes, we should run **Update Diagram** (from the **Simulation** menu or by pressing *Ctrl + D*).

Now we've finished our first model. It's time to see how it behaves.

Step 9 – do a first simulation

Let's see how our controller works in an open loop (without actually anything to control).

We must delete the input and output ports from the root level, since we're replacing them with appropriate **Sources** and **Sinks** blocks from the **Library Browser**.

We'll take the following blocks from the Simulink Library Browser:

- A **Constant** block (from **Simulink | Sources**) to be connected to the Vehicle speed input with the Constant value set to 0

- A **Step** block (from **Simulink | Sources**) to be connected to the Target speed input with the Final value set to 0.1 (remember that the throttle is clamped between 0 and 1)

- A **Scope** block (from **Simulink | Sinks**) to be connected to the Throttle output

We should have the system looking like the following screenshot:

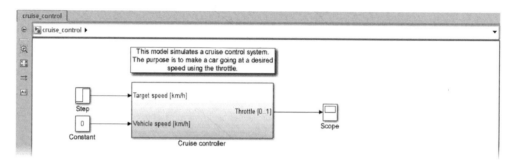

Running the simulation is an easy task: just click on the green **Run** button in the toolbar, or click the **Simulation | Run** menu entry, or type the *Ctrl + T* keyboard shortcut.

When the simulation is completed (the status bar at the bottom left shows the **Ready** word again), double click on the newly added **Scope** block and you'll see this neat graph:

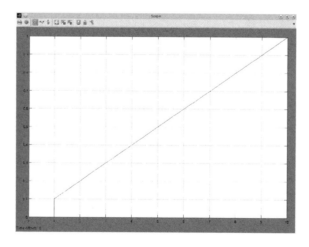

To make the graph fill the whole window size, press the **Autoscale** icon button (the sixth from the left).

Good! Notice that the simulation stopped at the tenth second; it is the default simulation time, which can be adjusted in the Simulink toolbar (right above the model editor).

We can do our little result analysis:

- Before **1** second: the target speed is still **0**, equal to the vehicle speed with no throttle required.

- At **1** second: the target speed (and the speed difference) goes to 0.1, the proportional factor of the PI controller kicks in and sets a throttle equal to the speed difference multiplied by K_p, while the integral factor starts working.

- From **1** second onwards: the proportional contribution to the throttle stays at 0.1, but the integral contribution rises linearly (K_i being 1, the slope of the throttle is equal to the speed difference, that is, 0.1).

A new variable has appeared in the workspace: tout. It is an array containing the time instants where the results have been calculated. By using the **Sinks | To Workspace** block, we can save the simulation results in the workspace too. This is often useful to do further analysis and prepare a report using MATLAB's powerful plotting functions, thus overcoming the limitations of the **Scope** block.

You can see that the resulting scope graph is not really continuous by opening the **'Scope' parameters** window [click on the **Parameters** icon button (the second from the left)] and choosing a line marker (**Line:**) in the **Style** tab. Simulink automatically chose an adequate time step. We'll discuss simulation times in the next chapter.

What we have just performed is an open-loop simulation: we have a controller running without the controlled system, so the speed (or better: the error **e(t)** that the controller is reacting to) is made up with a **Step** block. The purpose of open-loop simulations is to demonstrate and check the controller behavior with certain kinds of inputs.

What now? We need a mathematical model of a controlled system in order to perform a closed-loop simulation and see how our cruise controller is able to make the speed difference disappear by commanding the throttle. We need to model a car.

Our second model – the Alfa Romeo 147 GTA

With what we've learned so far, we're ready to develop a simple mathematical model of a real car in order to test and fine-tune the controller in a closed-loop simulation.

Luckily enough, a lot of technical detail is available nowadays on almost every car. The author likes the Alfa Romeo 147 GTA a lot, so the choice is made.

Open a new Simulink model and save it as alfa147gta.slx. The model will have one input (the throttle, coming from the cruise controller) and one output (the car's speed, going to the cruise controller).

We're interested only in the longitudinal speed (a car going straight on a flat ground), and we assume the gearbox to be ideal (shifting gears in no time).

How do we compute the speed?

Getting the speed – Newton's laws

We know that the car's speed is the integral of the acceleration in time:

$$v(t) = \int_0^t a(\tau)d\tau$$

Newton's second law reminds us that the acceleration is proportional to the total force applied on the car, with the mass **m** being the factor:

$$F(t) = m \times a(t) \rightarrow a(t) = \frac{F(t)}{m}$$

Since we're building a simplified model, we'll consider only the following three main forces:

- The engine force F_{Engine}, generated by the fuel burning in the engine
- The aerodynamic drag F_{Drag}, generated by the car moving in the air (that is, a viscous fluid)
- The rolling resistance F_{Res}, the sum of all the rolling frictions that oppose the movement

Putting it all together, we have:

$$v(t) = \int_0^t \frac{F(\tau)}{m} d(\tau)$$

$$F(t) = F_{Engine}(t) - F_{Drag}(t) - F_{Res}(t)$$

The mass being a constant, we can declare it in the workspace right away. The Alfa 147 GTA weighs 1360 kg, so we'll enter the following command in MATLAB's main window:

```
Mass = 1360;
```

Let's make the relevant blocks in the root system. Open **Library Browser** and drag three **Subsystem** blocks into the model (one for each force applied) from the **Ports & Subsystems** blockset; one **Add** block and one **Divide** block from the **Math Operations** blockset; one **Integrator** block from the **Continuous** blockset; and one **Constant** block from the **Sources** blockset for the mass.

Since we'll be working with the international metric system inside this model, we'll put a **Gain** block too (from the **Math Operations** blockset) before the output, to convert the speed unit from m/s to the one used by the cruise controller, km/h.

Rename the **Subsystem** blocks to **Aerodynamic drag**, **Rolling Resistance**, and **Engine Force**, and align them vertically.

Double-click on the **Add** block and edit the list of signs; we need three inputs, only one positive (the engine force). Let's keep the positive input as the last; the list of signs should be `--+`.

Double-click on the **Constant** block and set its **Constant value** parameter to `Mass` (the variable we just created in the workspace).

The same must be done for the **Gain** block, setting the Gain to `3.6` in order to convert from m/s to km/h.

After putting a brief note, connecting the blocks following the above formulas, and renaming the blocks, we should have our model as shown in the following screenshot:

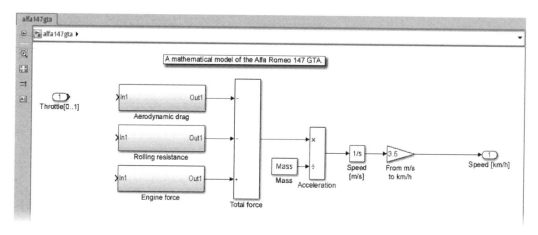

We still need to compute the forces. We'll start with the drag and the rolling resistance first, since they're simpler; then we'll build the algorithm calculating the engine force.

The aerodynamic drag equation

The aerodynamic drag force, whose effect is evident at high vehicle speeds, can be calculated with the drag equation as follows:

$$F_{Drag}(t) = K_{Drag} \times v^2(t) = \frac{1}{2}\rho C_D A \times v^2(t)$$

K_{Drag} is a constant for the car, made of:

- The air density ρ, at 20 °C and 101.325 kPa equals to 1.2041 kg/m³
- The drag coefficient C_D, which is 0.32 for the 147 GTA
- The frontal area A, approx. 2.2 m²

Let's declare it in the workspace with the following command:

```
Kdrag = 0.5 * 1.2041 * 0.32 * 2.2;
```

Since the vehicle speed needs to be an input of the block, we're adding a **Goto** and **From** block from the **Signal Routing** blockset to the root block.

The **Goto** and **From** blocks can avoid drawing a connection between two or more subsystems and are extremely helpful to avoid cluttering the view. It's a common practice in the automotive industry to use them instead of connecting input and output ports directly to the subsystems implementing the logic. When the system becomes too complex and there are many tags, it's helpful to assign the same foreground/background color to matching **Goto** and **From** blocks. This can be done by right-clicking on the block and using the **Format** menu option.

Open both and use the same tag: **speed**. It's suggested to hide their names. Be careful to connect the Goto block at the end of the integrator—we want the speed in m/s, not in km/h.

The root system should be looking like the following screenshot:

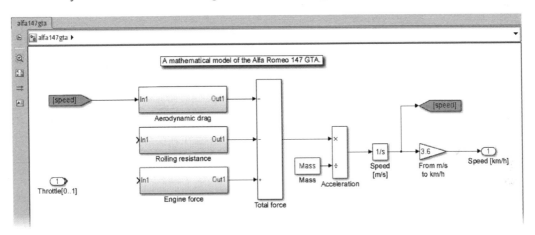

Inside the **Aerodynamic drag** subsystem, we'll implement the drag equation with one **Gain** block, one **Math function** block (both from **Simulink | Math Operations**), and one **Constant** block (from **Simulink | Sources**).

We'll use `Kdrag` as the **Gain** parameter for the **Gain** block and select the **pow** function in the **Math function** block (double-click and set the **Function** drop-down list to **pow**). A second input will appear; it is the exponential to apply; we'll connect it to the **Constant** block and set its **Constant value** parameter to 2.

Finally, we'll rename and connect the input and output ports, the input being the speed (in m/s) and the output being the drag force (in N). After making the connections, the subsystem should look like the following:

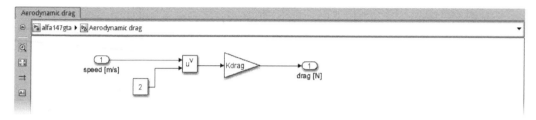

Don't forget to copy and connect the **speed** Goto in the parent system to the input port.

Let's do the next step, the rolling resistance.

The rolling resistance approximation

The rolling resistance (sometimes called rolling friction or rolling drag) is proportional to the vehicle speed. It's the main resistance at a lower speed.

It's not simple to obtain a precise formula because it involves knowledge about the tire characteristics, but we can simplify the calculations by assuming that:

- At approximately 30 m/s (100 km/h), the rolling resistance and the drag are equal

- The proportional factor is constant at other speeds

This assumption is valid for most cars.

So we can find, with v = 30 m/s, the constant K_{Res}:

$$F_{Res} = K_{Res} \times v = K_{Res} \times 30$$

$$F_{Drag} = K_{Drag} \times v^2 = K_{Drag} \times 30^2$$

$$F_{Res} = F_{Drag} \Rightarrow K_{Res} \times 30 = K_{Drag} \times 30^2 \Rightarrow K_{Res} = 30 \times K_{Drag}$$

K_{Res} being just 30 times bigger than K_{Drag}, we don't even need to declare a new variable in the workspace.

The implementation is simple: we just put inside the **Rolling resistance** subsystem a **Gain** block set to `30*Kdrag` and connect it to the input and output ports (renamed as usual). We should have this subsystem:

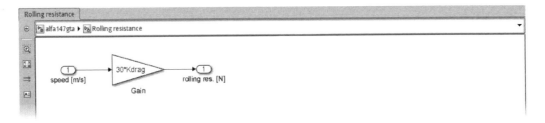

Don't forget to copy and connect the **speed** Goto in the parent system to the input port.

So far, so good. Now comes the hard part: the subsystem that calculates the engine force requested by the cruise controller (via the throttle input).

The engine force – engine, wheels, and transmission

Every combustion engine has a characteristic torque curve (also called lug curve) that can be found in almost every technical review book. The Alfa 147 GTA shows the following one:

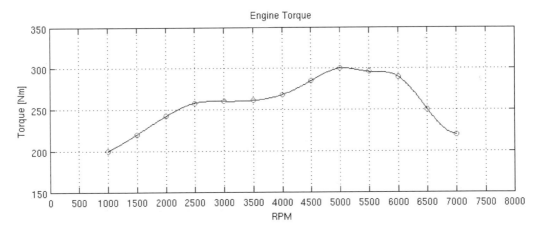

The torque in the preceding graph represents the maximum available torque τ_{MAX} (with the throttle fully open), measured at the crankshaft.

The engine and the wheels are linked together through the gearbox and the differential; the former applies a variable gear ratio K_{Gear} and the latter applies a constant final ratio K_{Final}.

Since we have to transform the vehicle speed to engine RPM first and the engine torque to the engine force last, all taking into account the gearbox and differential combined ratios, we need to model four subsystems:

- **Gearbox and differential**, will output the transmission ratio at the current speed
- **Wheel to RPM**, will output the current RPM based on the current transmission ratio and the current speed
- **Engine**, will receive the throttle command and output the resulting torque at the current RPM
- **Torque to force**, will convert the engine torque to the force that the engine is applying on the car

Let's start by having two input ports (the vehicle speed and the throttle input), one output port (the engine force), and the four empty **Subsystem** blocks (found in **Simulink | Ports & Subsystems**) in the **Engine force** subsystem. The subsystem should now look like the following screenshot:

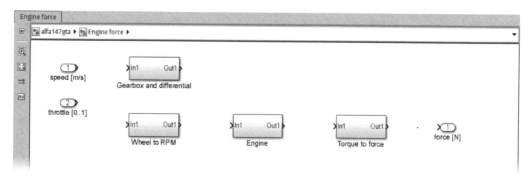

The first subsystem we'll implement is **Gearbox and differential**.

Gearbox and differential

From the crankshaft to the wheel, the rotation is reduced twice: first in the gearbox, where the reduction ratio can be changed by upshifting/downshifting, then in the differential, which has a fixed reduction ratio.

We need to implement an automatic gearbox; the simplest is the one that chooses the gear based on the current speed and doesn't have the reverse gear.

In the following table, we'll find the Alfa 147 GTA optimal speed ranges for each gear, together with the gear ratio K_{Gear}:

Gear	Speed range [km/h]	Gear ratio
1	< 39	3.500
2	39 – 59	2.235
3	60 – 86	1.520
4	86 – 109	1.156
5	110 – 129	0.971
6	≥ 130	0.818

The differential on the Alfa 147 GTA applies a final ratio K_{Final} of 3.733..

As an example: in the first gear, the engine's crankshaft is rotating 13 times (3.5*3.733) faster than the wheel axis, while in sixth gear, it's only three times (0.818*3.733) faster.

We'll put this data right now in the workspace by executing these commands:

```
GearRatio = [3.500 2.235 1.520 1.156 0.971 0.818];

FinalRatio = 3.733;
```

Let's build the automatic gearbox; the input is the vehicle speed in m/s, which gets converted to km/h through a **Gain** block with the value set to 3.6.

Then we'll use a particular construct to select the gear: an **If** block from the **Ports & Subsystems** blockset. The **If** block allows us to replicate exactly the C language's if()...elseif()...else construct. Opening the block parameters window reveals that we have to set the first if() condition: then we can define as many elseif() conditions as we like.

Looking at the speed ranges, it's easy to set the parameters:

- The **Number of inputs** will be set to 1, since we only need to evaluate the vehicle speed (the corresponding label inside the block will be **u1**)
- The **If expression** will be u1 < 39 (the first gear)
- The **Elseif expressions** elements will be u1 < 60, u1 < 86, u1 < 110, u1 < 130 (gears 2 through 5)
- The **Show else** condition checkbox will be checked (the sixth gear)

If we entered the parameters correctly, we should have the following subsystem now:

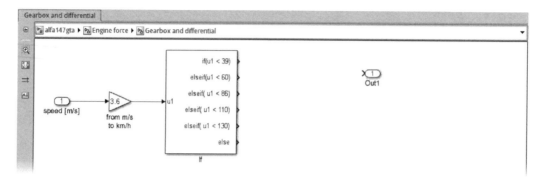

For each output of the **If** block, we need to put one **If Action Subsystem** (available in the **Ports & Subsystems** blockset). These subsystems must contain the code to be executed when the corresponding condition in the **If** block is verified (they're called conditionally executed subsystems). In our case, they'll output the chosen gear number. We don't need the input port; remove it from each one of these subsystems using a **Constant** block with the gear number instead.

In the following screenshot, we can see how the subsystem looks after inserting and editing the **If Action Subsystem** relative to the first gear and running the **Simulation | Update Diagram** action (the keyboard shortcut is *Ctrl + D*):

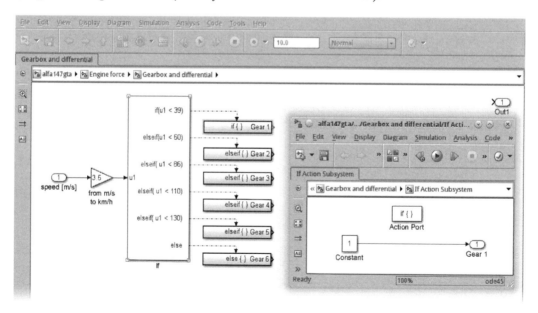

Notice that the connections between the **If** block and the subsystems are dotted. This means that the connection is not transporting a signal, but it's a function-call. When a condition is verified, the **If** block will call the subsystem connected to the corresponding port, executing its code.

To avoid Simulink emitting warnings in MATLAB's main window, the output ports of every conditionally executed subsystem should have the initial output value set in their parameters window.

We now have six possible gear values; how to put them together? We must use another particular block: the **Merge** block from the **Signal Routing** blockset. This block will instruct the connected subsystems to write their outputs to the same signal.

Let's put one **Merge** block into our model and open the parameters window by double-clicking on it. Since we have six subsystems, we need to set its **Number of inputs** parameter to 6, then connect each subsystem to one of the inputs.

The resulting model should be the one shown as follows:

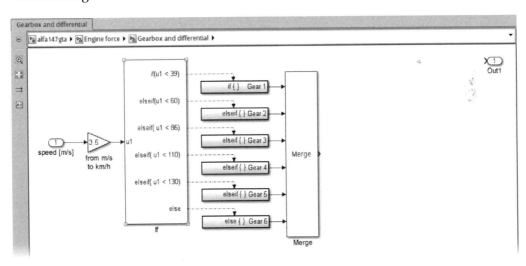

Now that we have the gear, we must use it to select the gear ratio.

We'll use **Direct Lookup Table (n-D)** (from **Simulink | Lookup Tables**). Open the parameters window, set the **Number of table dimensions** parameter to 1 and the **Table data** parameter to GearRatio. Since the table must be accessed with a zero-based index, we must subtract one unit from the gear number coming from the **Merge** block.

The subsystem and the **Direct Lookup Table** parameters are shown in the following screenshot:

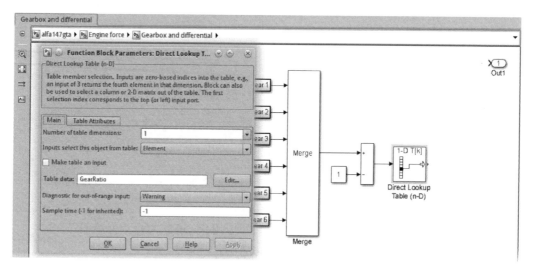

The last step is to include the final ratio due to the differential. That's easily done by putting a **Gain** block right before the output port (that should be renamed), and setting its **Gain** parameter to `FinalRatio`.

The final **Gearbox and differential** subsystem is shown in the following screenshot:

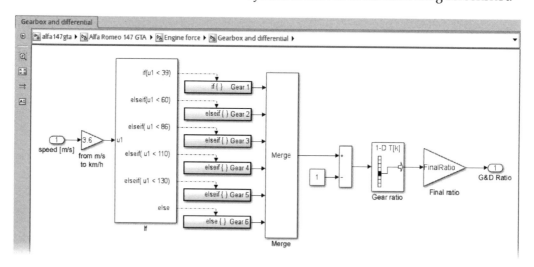

This subsystem's output will be used to convert the vehicle speed to the engine RPM, and later the engine torque to the new vehicle speed.

Wheel to RPM

The purpose of this subsystem is to get the engine RPM using two inputs: the vehicle speed, and the combined (gear and differential) reduction ratio.

The vehicle speed **v** can be translated to the rotational speed of the wheel (in RPM, revolutions per minute). The RPM_{Wheel} is equal to the distance the car has traveled in 60 seconds (v*60), divided by the wheel diameter (that is, 2π times the wheel radius r_{Wheel}).

Then we know that the engine and the wheels are linked together through the gearbox and the differential. We already have their ratios; the engine's RPM_{Engine} is equal to RPM_{Wheel} multiplied by the gear and differential ratios.

This gives us these easy formulas to implement in Simulink:

$$RPM_{Wheel} = \frac{v \times 60}{2\pi r_{Wheel}}$$

$$RPM_{Engine} = RPM_{Wheel} \times Ratio_{Gear} \times Ratio_{Differential} = \frac{v \times 60}{2\pi r_{Wheel}} \times Ratio_{G+D}$$

The Alfa Romeo 147 GTA requires 185/45R17 tires, meaning that:

- The wheel rim diameter is 17 in = 0.4318 m
- The tire section height is 45% of 185 mm ≈ 83.3 mm

So the wheel radius is 0.4318/2 + 0.0833 = 0.2992 m. Let's save it into the workspace with this command:

```
WheelRadius = 0.2992;
```

The subsystem's implementation in Simulink following the preceding formula is simple, using the well-known **Gain**, **Divide**, and **Product** blocks:

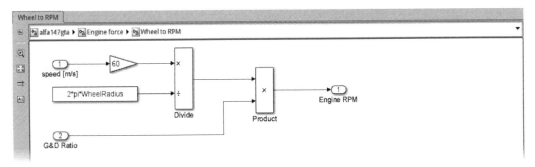

Now that we have the engine RPM, we can model the Engine subsystem.

Engine

This subsystem will calculate the engine torque response τ_{Engine}. The inputs are the engine RPM coming from the previous subsystem, and the throttle command from the cruise control system. The formula is very simple:

$$\tau_{Engine} = \tau_{MAX} \times \textit{Throttle}$$

In order to obtain the maximum torque τ_{MAX} available at a certain RPM, we need an interpolating block using the following coordinates (taken from the torque curve we saw earlier in this chapter):

RPM	1000	1500	2000	2500	3000	3500	4000	4500	5000	5500	6000	6500	7000
τ_{MAX}	200	220	242	258	260	261	268	285	300	296	290	250	220

Let's add these vectors to the workspace:

```
EngineRPM = [1000 1500 2000 2500 3000 3500 4000 4500 5000 5500
6000 6500 7000];

EngineTRQ = [200 220 242 258 260 261 268 285 300 296 290 250 220];
```

We'll place into the **Engine** subsystem a **1-D Lookup Table** (from **Simulink | Lookup Tables**), double-click on it, and configure it as follows:

- **Table dimensions**: 1 (for each RPM value, we only need one torque value)
- **Table data**: EngineTRQ (the ordinates)
- **Breakpoints 1**: EngineRPM (the abscissas)
- **Interpolation method** (in **Algorithm** tab): **Cubic spline** (how to calculate the curve between two known points)
- **Extrapolation method** (in **Algorithm** tab): **Linear** (how to calculate the curve outside the RPM range)

The **Engine** subsystem implementation will look like the following screenshot:

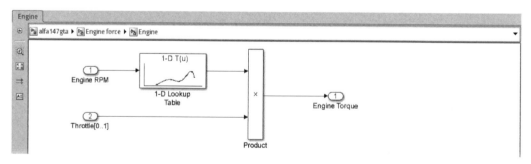

Easy, wasn't it? Now that we have the resulting τ_{Engine} we can calculate the force that the engine is applying to the vehicle in the next subsystem.

Torque to force

This subsystem converts the provided engine torque τ_{Engine} to the force F applied to the vehicle.

Thanks to Newton's third law, we know that the same force **F** is applied by the wheels on the ground. Remembering the definition of torque, we can relate F to the wheel torque τ_{Wheel} and the latter to the engine torque by applying the gear and differential ratios:

$$\tau_{Wheel} = F \times r_{Wheel}, \; \tau_{Wheel} = \tau_{Engine} \times Ratio_{G+D}$$

$$\Rightarrow F = \frac{\tau_{Engine} \times Ratio_{G+D}}{r_{Wheel}}$$

The Simulink implementation of the preceding formula is easily done with the now familiar **Product**, **Divide**, and **Constant** (set to `WheelRadius`) blocks, like in the following screenshot:

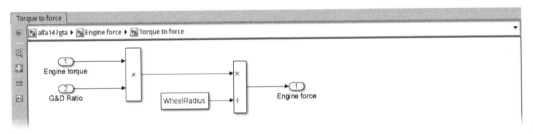

As always, don't forget to update the relevant connections in the parent subsystems.

The finishing touches

First of all, let's group all the root-level subsystems into one subsystem called **Alfa Romeo 147 GTA**, and save the current workspace as `alfa147gta.mat` since we've declared every constant we need.

 Like we did for the cruise controller model, we can have the model load the workspace automatically by setting its **PreLoadFcn** callback to: `load('alfa147gta.mat')`

Then we'll check if we did everything right by running a **Simulation |
Update Diagram** (*Ctrl + D*). The resulting root subsystem should look like the
following screenshot:

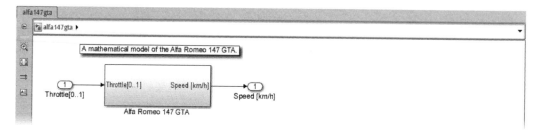

That's it! We managed to create a fully usable, fairly accurate car model!
Well, we can't steer, but we can surely have drag races!

Summary

We've now learned the basics of building continuous time models implementing
ordinary differential equations, together with almost every modeling technique
you'll ever need.

In the next chapter, we'll be discussing the simulation phase using the models and
workspaces we've just created.

3
Simulating a Model

In this chapter, we'll learn how to simulate a model. We'll start with a little theory about the solver and simulation time in order to understand the main concepts behind the Simulink engine. Then we will assemble the test system by putting together the cruise controller and the car model, and run various simulations. We'll be able to calibrate our cruise controller and we'll learn what really sets Simulink apart—many different source blocks and one mighty sink block, Scope.

The mandatory theory

Before starting the simulation, we'll have a closer look at how Simulink computes the simulation results, in order to be able to choose the appropriate simulation time and solver.

Let's build a simple system that finds the solution to this problem:

$$y'(t) = -y(t), y(0) = 1$$

The exact mathematical solution is $y(t) = e^{-t}$.

The Simulink model (which we'll save as `example.slx`) that implements the problem is:

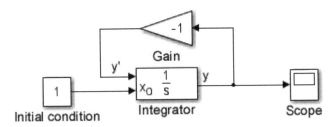

Notice that we've set the **Initial condition source** parameter of the **Integrator** block to be **external**.

To configure the simulation time and solver of this model, click on the **Model Configuration Parameters** option from the **Simulation** menu (keyboard shortcut: *Ctrl + E*).

A new window will open; select the **Solver** node from the left-side panel, which will give you access to configure the **Solver options** and **Simulation time** parameters.

Under the **Solver options** section, select the **Type** list value as **Fixed-step** (don't worry, we'll explain the meaning later) as shown in the following screenshot:

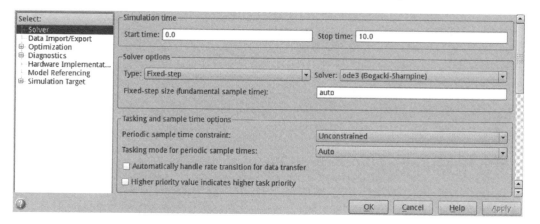

Then let's edit the Scope block parameters. We want to see where Simulink does the calculations, so we'll click on the **Style** tab and set the **Marker** option as round to both lines:

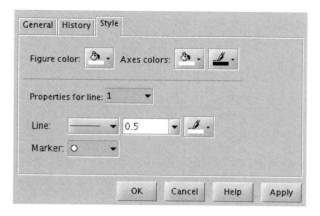

Now that we have set up our example, let's begin by examining the simulation times.

The simulation times – when the math is done

There are three main times to be set before starting with the simulation: the simulation start time, the simulation stop time, and the simulation step size.

The **Start time** and **Stop time** parameters under **Simulation time** are self-explanatory; they tell Simulink the time period (in seconds) required to perform the simulation. Usually **Start time** is set to **0.0**, and **Stop time** to either `inf` (meaning that the simulation will never end until it's stopped by the user) or a time when the transient effects in the model become negligible. The default value of **Stop time** is **10.0**.

The step size defines the time period that Simulink uses to sample the inputs and calculate the outputs. The default value is set to `auto`; that is, Simulink will try to determine the appropriate step size.

Let's run the simulation and see the result by double-clicking on the **Scope** block. We should see this graph:

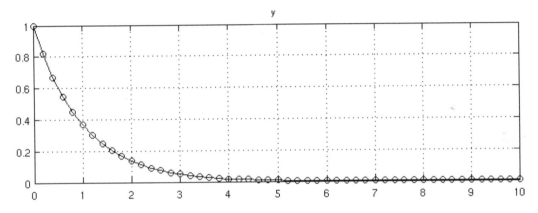

By zooming in on the graph a little, we'll find that the samples have been computed every 0.2 seconds (**0.2, 0.4, 0.6,** and so on). This is confirmed by the warning that Simulink issued in MATLAB's **Command Window**, which is seen as follows:

```
Warning: Unable to determine a fixed step size based on the sample times
in the model 'example', because the model does not have any discrete
sample times. Picking a fixed step size of (0.2) based on simulation
start and stop times.
```

Let's take a quick note of the result at 1 second: it is $y(1) = 0.3677$.

The exact solution is $e^{-1} = -0.3679$, so the simulation result is fairly accurate.

Now, in the **Model Configuration Parameters** window, let's set **Fixed-step size (fundamental sample time)** as 1, and run the simulation again.

You'll be presented with this graph:

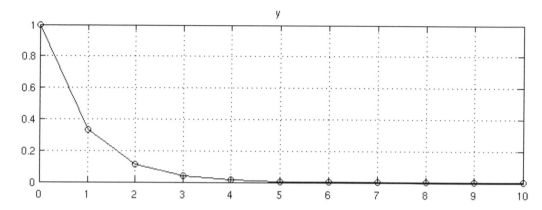

What happened? We told Simulink to acquire new samples every second; thus, the resulting curve is less accurate. If we look at the result for 1 second, we can see that it has changed to $y(1) = -0.3333$. With such a large step size, we shouldn't be surprised that the solution Simulink found is showing a greater difference from the exact one.

Most of the time, your models will give unpredictable results because you chose an inadequately long step size. Vice versa, you may have defined a very small time step size, just to be on the safe side, and your simulation could take ages. If you've got a fast computer, try setting a step size of 0.00001 and running the simulation again (you'll have to uncheck the **Limit data points to last** option in the **Scope** parameter window under the **History** tab).

 The rule of thumb is to have a time step smaller than half the smallest period of your analog signals if the system is not stiff like this one — more about that in the later sections.

The solvers – these great unknown

The solvers are the answers to the question: how does Simulink run the simulation?

Every solver performs the simulation by advancing one time step and computing the new outputs starting from the previous state(s) of the system until the end of the simulation time. The initial system state must be fully defined.

The appropriate solver for a model can be chosen by defining these characteristics:

- Time step size, which can be fixed or variable
- Presence of continuous states in the system
- Stiffness of the system

Variable-step versus fixed-step solvers

A variable-step solver will choose to use a shorter time step when the signal derivative is changing faster in order to obtain a better approximation, while it will use a longer step when the result changes at a slower pace. The most used variable-step solver is the **ode45** solver (this is the default Simulink solver as well).

A fixed-step solver will, on the other hand, always use the same step size. The simplest is the **ode1** solver (the famous Euler method).

We've already run our example with a fixed-step solver. Let's change this to a variable-step solver by opening the **Model Configuration Parameters** window and setting the **ode45** solver.

We now have the option to configure more **Solver** parameters; we'll allow it to use a **Max step size** of 1 second and a **Min step size** of 0.2 seconds, setting other parameters to the default value. Running the simulation now will give us the following result:

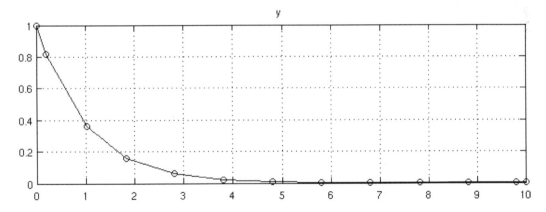

We can see that the step size is indeed variable: the second value has been computed after only 0.2 seconds, and then the step size grew bigger and stayed at 1 second. We got a good approximation in the problematic region while using longer steps in the almost constant region, thus achieving a faster simulation time than a fixed-step solver with a step size of 0.2 seconds.

But how does the solver determine when it's necessary to reduce the step size? The answer is by looking at the tolerances defined in the **Model Configuration Parameters** window.

Relative tolerance defines the maximum error as a percentage of the actual value. The default value (`1e-3`) means that an error of 0.1 percent is accepted.

Absolute tolerance defines the maximum error as a scalar value. When it is set to `auto`, Simulink will assume `1e-6` initially (that is, `0.000001`), then change it to the maximum error calculated with the relative tolerance.

The **Shape preservation** option, off (**Disable all**) by default, helps to increase the accuracy when the solution's derivative varies rapidly at the cost of a more computing-intensive simulation (thus increasing the overall time to compute the result).

Finally, there's the option **Number of consecutive min steps**, which defines how many times the solver can use a time step smaller than the minimum step size violations defined before issuing a warning or an error.

Let's set the **Relative tolerance** parameter to `1e-5` and run the simulation. We'll obtain this result:

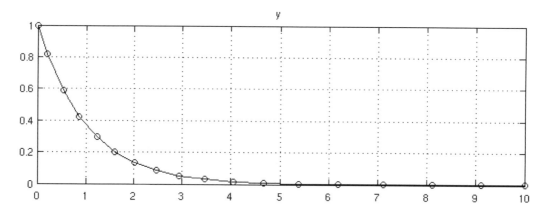

This time, the solver chose to use more shorter steps while the signal was changing to improve the accuracy, thanks to the relative tolerance we've set; then the step size grew gradually back to 1 second.

Variable-step solvers give us a good trade-off between result approximation and overall simulation times in models, whereas fixed-step solvers are too computationally intensive to be used efficiently.

 Fixed-step solvers are *required* for code generation and real-time control purposes because Simulink can't go back in time to give a more accurate result.

Continuous versus discrete

A system can be continuous or discrete based on the presence of integrators or derivatives in the model (these are called continuous states). In other words, if the system is represented by the means of one or more differential equations, the system is continuous. Our cruise controller is continuous because it has an integral component.

The continuous solver can choose to perform several iteration cycles in a single time step to reach the best possible approximation of the final result. Such solvers fall into the **ODE (Ordinary Differential Equation** solvers) category.

If a system is discrete, there are no differential equations but only memories and mathematical operands. A discrete solver is unable to perform the numerical integration required by continuous states.

The continuous system requires continuous solvers, while Simulink will switch to a discrete solver for discrete systems even if a continuous solver has been specified.

Try to set a discrete solver in our example system and run a simulation. An error window will appear, telling us that a discrete solver can't be used because the model contains continuous states.

Stiff versus nonstiff

In a stiff continuous system, certain solvers are unable to compute the result unless the step size is small enough; thus, a stiff solver is needed. These systems can be identified by an overall slowly changing solution that can vary rapidly in a very small time period.

Our example is mildly stiff: the ode45 solver had to use a small step size to compute the result close to t = 0, but it managed to get the job done by changing the time step. A more appropriate choice would have been the **ode23t** solver (moderately stiff), which would have given the following result:

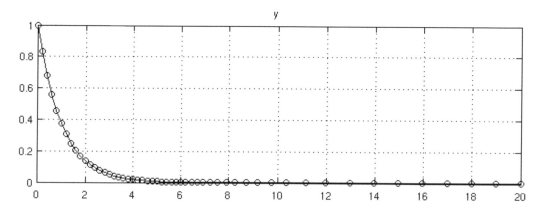

Let's choose another nonstiff solver, the fixed-step **ode1**, implementing the Euler method. Set the **Fixed step size** parameter to 1.5 and run the simulation:

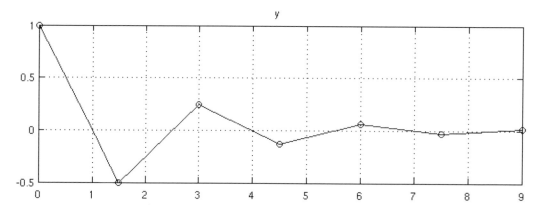

That's interesting: Using the Euler method with a long time step shows the result to be oscillating around the mathematical result, but the solution is still convergent.

Setting the step size to 2 seconds will show that it can't converge anymore, and any step size higher than 2 seconds will make the simulation diverge from the correct result and go towards infinite oscillation. The following figure shows the result with a step size of 2.1 and a simulation time of 20 seconds:

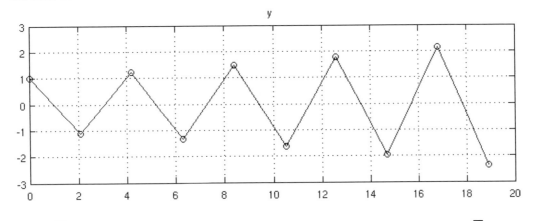

The following article presents stiff solvers in a way that is easy to understand: http://blogs.mathworks.com/ seth/2012/07/03/why-do-we-need-stiff- ode-solvers/.

The documentation center, accessible by pressing *F1*, has detailed information about the solver types and parameters. This information can be found by navigating to **Simulink | Simulation | Configure simulation**.

Now that we've learned how solvers work and how to choose the right solver, we can start with the practice.

Build the complete closed-loop system

So far we've got two models: a simple cruise controller and a beautiful car. Until now, they've been treated separately in an open loop. Remembering what we learned in the previous chapter, we're going to place the required blocks and connect them in a closed loop.

Let's open both the models and copy them to a new model named `cruise_control_ sim.slx`. If their workspaces aren't loaded automatically, load them by dragging them from their folders to the MATLAB's **Command Window** and save the new workspace as `cruise_control_sim.mat`. It's suggested to have the new workspace loaded automatically via the PreLoadFcn model callback as we have learned in the previous chapter.

In order to see what's happening inside the engine, let's pull out the **Gear** and **RPM** signals from **Alfa Romeo 147 GTA | Engine force | Gearbox and differential** until we reach the root block, by adding and connecting the output ports to every parent subsystem.

Then we need to make the important connections: the **Throttle** output of the **Cruise controller** system has to be connected to the **Throttle** input of the **Alfa Romeo 147 GTA** system. The same goes for the **Speed** port, going from the car to the controller.

We need to place a **Scope** block to view the outputs too. This block will be placed near the upper-right corner of the root view above the systems.

In order to easily connect the signals to the **Scope** block, we'll use four *From* blocks paired with four *Goto* blocks. Three of the From blocks will be connected to the car's output, which are labeled using their names, while the fourth From block will be connected to the throttle signal and labeled as Throttle. The Goto blocks will be labeled the same way as the From blocks and placed near the **Scope** block.

Another couple of Goto/From blocks will be added to feed the remaining controller's input. The From block will be connected to the **Target speed** input of the controller, and the Goto block is placed above the systems near the upper-left corner of the root view. Both will be labeled as Target.

We now have a system, as shown in the following figure:

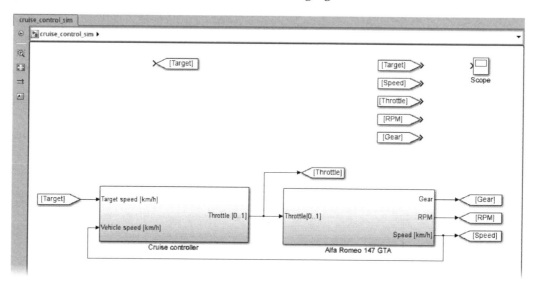

It's time to connect the From blocks, tagged, **Target, Speed, Throttle, RPM,** and **Gear,** to the **Scope** block.

To visualize the **Target** and **Speed** signals on the same **Scope** graph, rather than having them in separate graphs, we'll add a **Mux** block and connect these signals to it.

The Mux block creates a virtual bus containing the muxed signals, which must be of the same datatype. The subsequent blocks (connected to that virtual bus) will execute their operations on each virtual signal. This is extremely useful when you need to perform the same operations on many signals. The Demux block does the opposite operation; it pulls out the muxed signals in the same order that they were muxed.

The Bus Creator block may seem to be equivalent to the Mux block, but it serves different purposes. Unlike the Mux block, the Bus Creator block creates real buses (accepted only by bus-enabled blocks). The signals entering the bus must be named; they can be complex and have different datatypes. The Bus Creator block is used by code-generation tools to declare and populate C structs.

Open the **Scope** block configuration window and set the **Number of axes** to 4, then connect the signals from the Mux block and the **Throttle, RPM**, and **Gear** From blocks. Finally, give a name to each signal exiting the From blocks by double-clicking on the signal lines. Use the corresponding From block label as the signal name. The signal names will be displayed above the **Scope** block graphs.

The portion of the system connected to the **Scope** block should look like the following figure:

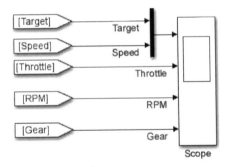

Another useful option of the **Scope** configuration is the **Legends** checkbox in the **General** tab. When this option is checked, a legend with the signal names will be printed in the graph window, allowing us to distinguish the **Speed** and **Target** signals easily.

We're now ready to race.

Configuring the simulation

First and foremost, with the knowledge we gained in this chapter, we have to choose the right simulation times, the solvers, and their options. Let's open the model's **Configuration Parameters** window (or press *Ctrl + E*) for the last time.

Simulation times

The **Start time** parameter will be left as 0.0 seconds. We're not going to wait at the car parking, are we?

Having a powerful engine, we'll reach the target speed of 100 km/h from standstill in less than 10 seconds. But we want to see how the vehicle speed settles to the target speed (to detect overshoots and make sure the target is actually reached), so we'll use a long enough **Stop time**, 50 seconds.

The step size will be large enough to allow an external (soft real-time) application to run synchronously but small enough to not allow the car to reach a speed higher than the target before the cruise control can cut the throttle. This happens when the target speed is low and the car is in the first gear and jumps from 0 to 20 km/h in less than 2 seconds. Therefore, we're choosing a step size of 0.1 seconds.

In a simulation of 50 seconds, we'll be getting 500 samples.

Remember that the **Scope** block is limited to 5000 samples by default with a step size smaller than 0.01 seconds we would have to edit or remove the **Limit data points to last** option in the 'Scope' parameters window under the **History** tab.

Solvers

Since we're going to test our cruise controller with an external application, we cannot use a variable-step solver; we have to choose a fixed-step solver.

It must be continuous since we've got three integrators (two in the cruise controller, and one in the car).

The system is mildly stiff: the throttle command, even if clamped, can vary very fast from 0 to 1 (depending on the K_p constant), and the speed signal can be problematic at lower speeds for the reasons we listed earlier.

Since K_p will not have a big value (otherwise, driving the car would be an unpleasant experience) and the chosen step size is small, the ode1 Euler solver is likely to work well, so we're using it.

Run our first serious simulation

Let's place a **Step** block in the model, connect it to the **Target** Goto (whose corresponding From block is connected to the **Target speed** controller input), and set its **Final value** to `100` km/h.

Run the simulation and open the **Scope** block. The speed graph should be like this one:

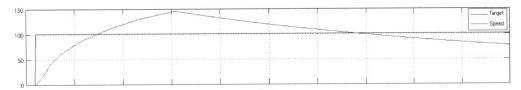

Quite an overshoot! The vehicle speed reaches almost 150 km/h when the controller closes the throttle. This is due to a too high integral gain, K_i, forcing the vehicle to go a lot faster than intended. Who wants a ride?

Calibrate the PI controller

To calibrate the PI controller constants, K_p and K_i, we'll use this manual method of keeping K_i to zero and finding the K_p value to where the **Throttle** signal begins to oscillate.

Then we'll halve the found value and save it into K_p and tune K_i in order to reach the target speed with a minimum overshoot.

Calibrating K_p

Prepare the model by setting K_i to zero with this MATLAB command: `Ki = 0`.

We'll start with an insanely high proportional gain value, `Kp = 5`. The result is shown in the following graphs:

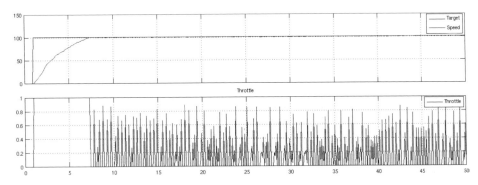

No doubt K$_p$ is too high (oscillations are strong); no one would accept a ride from us.

Let's try with `Kp = 1.1`:

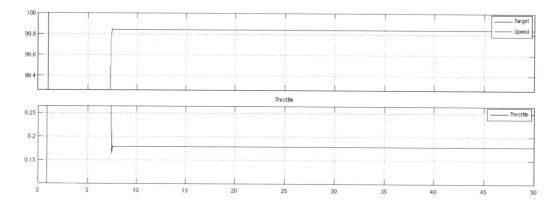

The preceding graph has been zoomed to show that there is only a small glitch due to the fact that the speed increased beyond the target speed in the middle of a sample period. But the rest of the graph shows no oscillations, so we're about to find the right value.

The next simulation is done with `Kp = 0.8`:

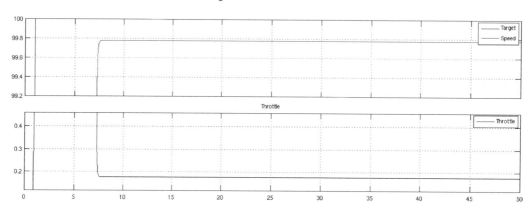

This works very well. We can assume our K$_p$ to be the half of 0.8. That's a fairly high value, but there aren't passengers in the car... yet!

Let's type the MATLAB command, `Kp = 0.4`, and save the workspace.

Calibrating K$_i$

Now we'll keep K$_p$ as the untouched constant and calibrate K$_i$. The purpose is to use the integral component to actually reach the target speed, keeping the overshoot below 1 percent of the target speed.

We've already seen that `Ki = 1` generates way too much overshoot, so we'll try much smaller values such as `Ki = 0.01`:

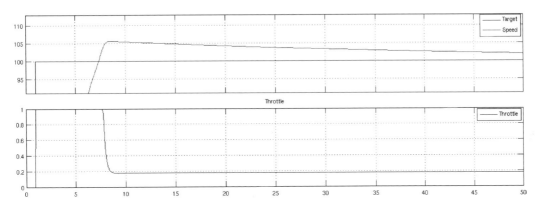

The overshoot is above 5 percent of the target speed, so we need to choose a lower K$_i$. Let's try with `Ki = 0.002`:

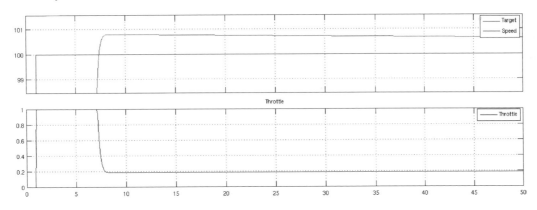

Got it! The overshoot is below 1 percent of the target speed.

We have now found both the calibration constants: `Kp = 0.4` and `Ki = 0.002`. Don't forget to save the workspace (`cruise_control_sim.mat`).

Test with other sources

So far we've learned how to use the **Step** source block. This is arguably the most important source because it presents clearly the system's transient answer to a stimulus.

But that's about it; it doesn't show the response to a wave, a random signal, or a noise.

A more thorough test with other sources could help us detect problems that were overlooked. For instance, we didn't take into account while testing that the car can show a very different response in lower gears: at 100 km/h, it was running in fourth gear.

Sine Wave

The cruise controller is acting only on the throttle, so we can predict that it will be hard for it to follow decreasing speeds.

Let's try using a **Sine Wave** block as the target speed source, which was configured as follows:

- **Bias**: 100 (km/h)
- **Amplitude**: 20 (km/h)
- **Frequency**: 0.2 (rad/s)

The simulation result is shown as follows:

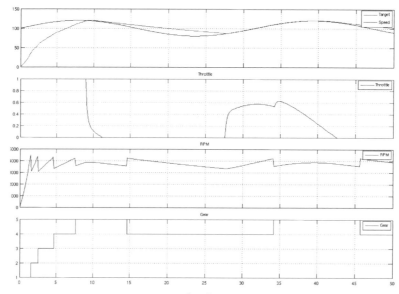

Our cruise controller can't use the brakes, so it isn't able to follow the falling side of the wave. But it's able to rise up fast from zero and follow the rising wave accurately.

Ramp

The **Ramp** block will give us a linear increase in speed to match. We could use it to observe the maximum speed the car is able to give us. Of course, at some point the car won't accelerate anymore because the opposing drag and rolling resistances will be equal to the force produced by the engine, and a maximum speed will be reached.

Let's try a slow-rising **Ramp** block using the following configuration:

- **Slope**: As we have a simulation time of 50 seconds, set the final target speed to 300 km/h. So the slope parameter will be 300/50 = 6 km/h per second. Enter this value (6) for this field.
- **Start time**: 0.
- **Initial output**: 0.

The result would look like this:

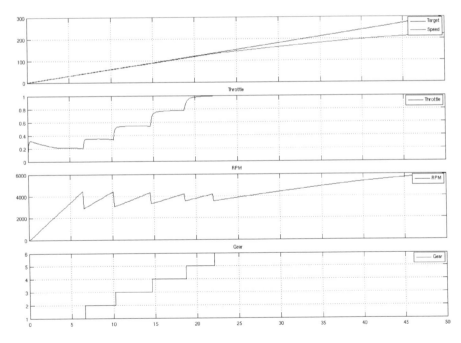

Everything looks in place: zooming in on the throttle and speed graphs when the car is in first gear doesn't reveal any problems so far.

Let's make a more thorough test using a configurable source: the signal builder block.

Signal Builder

The **Signal Builder** block allows you to create and edit your own signals through a supposedly intuitive graphical user interface. Once you put the **Signal Builder** block in the model and open it, you should see the following screenshot:

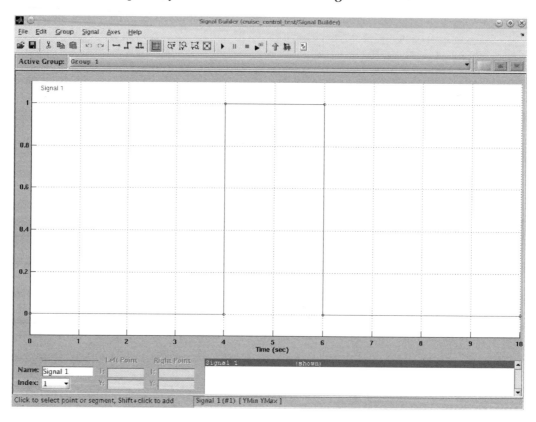

With the mouse you can:

- Drag the points up and down (but not right/left)
- Drag the vertical lines right and left
- Drag the horizontal/oblique lines up and down
- Open a fancy menu by right-clicking the mouse

That's all that you can do with the GUI. You may try to delete the signal, but Simulink will complain because this is the only signal in the block. The easiest way to make it work is to create a new signal.

First of all, increase the time range; we've got a 50 second simulation time and this block keeps the default of 10 seconds. To do so, navigate to **Axes | Change Time Range** as shown in the following screenshot and set **Max time** as 50:

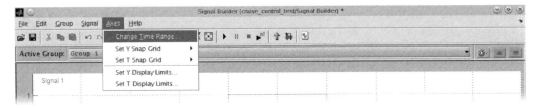

Then, create a new signal by navigating to **Signal | New | Custom...**, represented in the following screenshot:

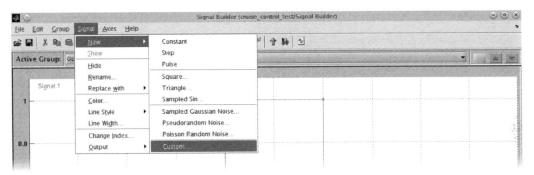

We'll have to insert **Time values** and **Y values**. Spending 5 seconds in lower gears, 10 seconds in higher gears, and using speeds slightly below the thresholds at which gear-shifting occurs, the strings to insert are:

Time values	[0 5 5 10 10 20 20 30 30 40 40 50]
Y values	[30 30 50 50 80 80 100 100 120 120 140 140]

Now that we've created another signal, we can safely delete the previous one and obtain the situation presented in the following screenshot:

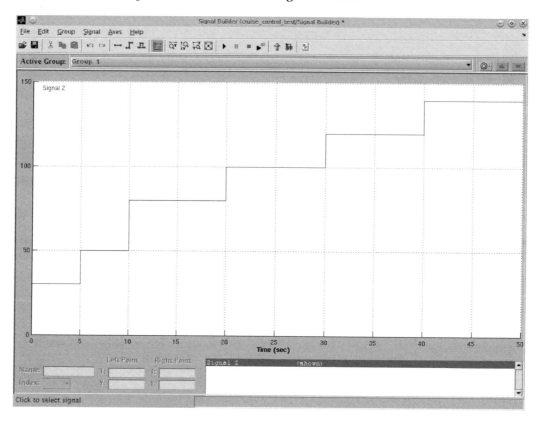

Let's connect it to the target speed Goto block input and run the simulation again. Now the **Scope** block will show the following result:

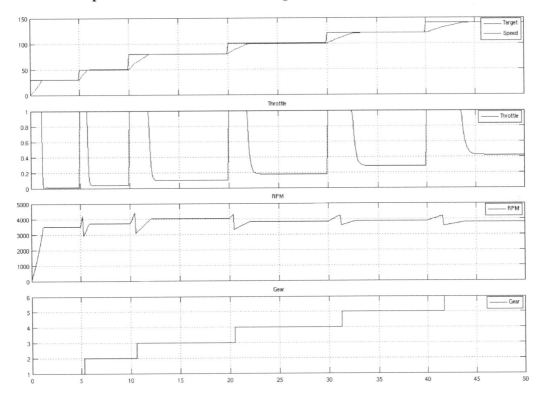

Again, we make sure that there are no problems by zooming in on the **Speed** and **Throttle** graphs.

Having found the right calibration constants, we can finally use our cruise controller on something more interesting than a model.

Summary

You are now able to prepare a Simulink virtual test bench and run the closed-loop simulations of a controller and the mathematical model of the controlled item by setting the right simulation parameters, choosing the most appropriate sources, and viewing the result on the **Scope** block.

In the next chapter, you'll learn how to use your Simulink models with something outside Simulink itself. Have you got a spare car?

4
Using the Model

In the earlier chapters we've developed a simple cruise controller model and the controlled car model, and then we've tested and fine-tuned the controller model. All the work has been done in Simulink only.

We couldn't perform our model testing on something other than the car model, because we still lack an interface with an external system, outside Simulink. This external system could be the real car for those lucky ones who have a spare 147 GTA in their garage and all the hardware needed to command its engine control unit, or — more realistically — a car simulation software like the one provided with this book.

In this chapter we'll take a first look at the software and understand how it is exchanging the data.

We'll then learn how to develop custom blocks to communicate with the application and use them with our cruise controller model. Those custom blocks will be developed with the MATLAB scripting language, which has the advantage of having a simple and intuitive syntax.

The final part of this chapter, aimed at those who know the C language, discusses the implementation of the same blocks using the C language.

The external software – a Qt5 application

The application is shipped with the code bundle provided with this chapter. It's located in the `external_app` folder (in code bundle), containing:

- The 64-bit Linux executable (`external_app/Linux/alfa147gta_linux64`), which needs the Qt5 libraries to be installed in the system (the package is usually called `qt5`) and must be marked as executable (by typing `chmod +x alfa147gta_linux64` in the terminal)

- The 32-bit Windows executable (`external_app\Windows\`
  `alfa147gta_win32.exe`) built using MinGW; the needed libraries
  (the `.dll` files) are located in the same folder to avoid you the hassle
  of installing Qt5 on Windows

- The source code (`external_app/source/alfa147gta`, distributed under
  the GPL license), made using Qt Creator

Move the application (and every `.dll` file, if you're on Windows) to the folder we'll
use as the MATLAB working folder, and run it by double-clicking on the icon.

You should see the following window:

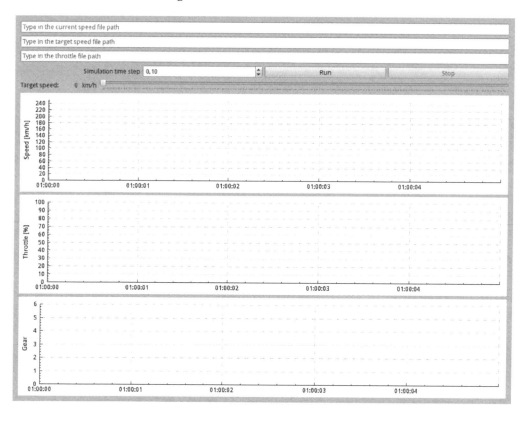

The application works by reading and writing three text files (whose paths have to
be put in the three input fields above the graphs), having only one line with a real
number. The vehicle speed and target speed files are written by the application itself,
while the throttle command file is read. Throughout this chapter, we'll assume the
files to be `speed.txt`, `target.txt`, and `throttle.txt`, located in the same directory
as the application itself. Enter their paths in the application input fields.

There is another input field: the simulation step size (in seconds). It must be set equal to the step size used by the cruise controller model, and allow the application to run synchronously with the model. The value we'll use, as discussed in the previous chapter, is 0.1 seconds.

Finally, the slider allows us to vary the target speed easily.

As soon as the **Run** button is clicked, the application begins simulating the vehicle (assuming an initial throttle input equal to 0) the same way our mathematical Alfa 147 GTA model did.

Try moving the target speed slider: you'll see a red line moving in the speed graph. Of course, since there isn't any controller writing the throttle file, the other graphs will keep their default values.

The first graph, displaying the speeds, will have two lines: the red one is the target speed, and the blue one is the vehicle speed, with the difference between the two highlighted in yellow. The second graph displays the throttle command and the third graph displays the the current gear.

The **Stop** button will stop the simulation. You'll notice that the speed.txt, target.txt, and throttle.txt files have been automatically created by the application itself.

At this point we know that in order to use this application we've got to develop two custom blocks: a sink block that will write a scalar, one-dimensional, real signal to a file, and a source block that will read a file and output a scalar, one-dimensional, real signal. Custom blocks are developed with **S-functions**.

The Swiss army knife – S-functions

S-functions are the most powerful way of defining custom blocks. There's no limit to what you can do: re-use an existing code, implement a functionality not available in your current blocksets, exchange data with external applications and devices, and so on. If you can code it, you can use it.

S-functions can be implemented using the following languages: the MATLAB scripting language, C/C++, and Fortran. S-functions written with the latter two need to be compiled first in order to produce a shared library loadable by the Simulink engine, while a MATLAB S-function will be interpreted and executed during the simulation.

In this chapter we'll focus on Level 2 MATLAB S-functions, since they are the easiest to develop even for people without programming knowledge. But the final part of this chapter, aimed at those who already know the C language, will explain how to obtain the same results with C MEX S-functions.

 There are Level 1 MATLAB S-functions too, with a different (older and likely to be deprecated soon) API to work with. New MATLAB S-functions should be developed using the Level 2 API.

In order to code an S-function, we'll have to learn some concepts: how a simulation is done, what information the Simulink engine requires, how S-functions provide that information, and how to store persistent data during the simulation.

The simulation phases

The whole simulation process can be divided into three phases: initialization, simulation, and cleanup.

The initialization phase takes place before the simulation starts: Simulink needs to know the number of inputs and outputs for each block (with their dimensions), the parameters, the sample time, and the amount of memory to be reserved. While some properties are read during model development (without knowing the number of input ports and output ports, the block could not be drawn), the required memory is allocated only once, as soon as the user starts the simulation.

The simulation loop is executed until the simulation reaches its end time, or the user manually stops it. Since block properties and memories have been properly set up in the previous phase, all that Simulink needs is to know how the outputs have to be calculated and update the memories.

Finally, the cleanup phase is executed only once, that is, after the simulation is stopped. During this phase, Simulink will free every system resource that has been allocated in the initialization phase, asking custom blocks what the appropriate method to free their resources is.

Level 2 MATLAB S-function callbacks

The S-function block must implement a certain number of predefined routines, or callbacks, that the Simulink engine will call during the three simulation phases.

Only two callbacks are required, the other ones being optional (if you don't need them, you don't have to declare them).

The mandatory callbacks

The first mandatory callback to have is the `setup` function called during the initialization phase. The block characteristics — inputs, outputs, sample times, and number of parameters — must be defined here. This function is called during model updates too (while developing the model).

There is an important configuration related to input ports: the direct feedthrough. If, at a given simulation time step, the current input port value is required to calculate one or more output, that port must have the direct feedthrough flag set.

If, on the other hand, the outputs can be calculated using only the previous states (memories, integrators), the direct feedthrough flag must be cleared for every input port.

This will allow the Simulink engine to determine the block execution order and detect the presence of algebraic loops: they occur when an input port with direct feedthrough is driven by the output of the same block, either directly, or by a feedback path through other blocks which have direct feedthrough. Memory and integrator blocks are capable of breaking the loop.

The second mandatory callback is the `Outputs` function, called in the simulation loop at each time step. This function implements the core logic of the block; its purpose is to calculate the output ports values using the block's memories (and input values, if the block has direct feedthrough).

That's it. Those are the required callbacks. But if you want to store some variables in a persistent memory (that will be available to every callback during the simulation), we'll need to use some optional callbacks too.

The most useful optional callbacks

These callbacks are the ones we should know about in order to save persistent data during the simulation.

The first optional callback, `PostPropagationSetup`, is the one where you declare the necessary memory. It will be executed once after the `setup` routine, when Simulink has calculated the datatype and the dimensions for each signal in the model.

The second optional callback, `Start`, is called right before the beginning of the simulation loop. It's used to assign an initial value to the memory declared in `PostPropagationSetup`.

The third optional callback, Update, serves the purpose of updating the persistent memory and it is called at every step in the simulation loop, immediately after Outputs.

The fourth optional callback, Terminate, belongs to the cleanup phase and must be used when some system resources allocated in PostPropagationSetup can't be freed automatically by Simulink (common examples are pipes, network sockets, and devices like an RS232 serial port; they have to be closed first).

> The Documentation center, as always, has a complete list of the available callbacks, with their description and example usage. It's under this path: **Simulink | Block creation | Host-specific code | MATLAB S-Functions | S-Function Callback Methods.**

The work vector – DWork

Let's suppose we would like to write a custom log-to-file block, which would save each input value to a line in a log file.

The implementation would be as follows:

- Open a file for writing in Start
- Write to the file each time Outputs is called
- Close the file in Terminate

Where could we store the file handle?

We can't store it in a local variable. A local variable will disappear as soon as the Start callback is completed, and the Outputs callback will throw an error at the first attempt to write some data.

We could store it in a workspace (global) variable. The file handle will be accessible to the Outputs and Terminate callbacks. But there's a huge problem: if we had more than one log-to-file blocks in the same model, they will use the same variable to store the file handles, therefore writing everything to the same file. To overcome this problem we may use a vector variable holding a list of open file handles, and a boilerplate code determining the right index to use for each log-to-file block. Quite difficult, not to mention memory management issues.

There's a much better, cleaner way: work vectors. Yes, The MathWorks wrote the boilerplate code for us. The DWork vector is a portion of memory the Simulink engine allocates for each S-function block that needs to store persistent data during simulation, solving the problem of concurrent access; every S-function block will use only its own memory. And that memory is managed directly by the Simulink engine. Isn't it sweet?

There are four types of DWork vectors:

- **Generic DWork** type vectors are the most generic, allowing to store variables, discrete states, and mode data

- **DState** type vectors are specifically made to store discrete states (memories), enabling Simulink's data logging facilities

- **Scratch** type vectors are persistent for only one time step; the data stored in them will disappear as soon as the next time step begins

- **Mode** type vectors can store switches modifying the S-function operating mode

 To understand what an S-function mode is, imagine a block calculating the absolute value of the input. It has two modes of operation: copy the unchanged input to the output or change the input sign before copying it to the output. By using zero-crossing detection, we could set the mode in a single-width Mode DWork vector, used later in the Outputs callback.

Using DWork vectors is simple. We must use the PostPropagationSetup callback to define:

- How many DWork vectors we need
- The type of each DWork vector
- The width of each DWork vector, equal to the number of elements we want to store
- The characteristics (datatype, complexity) of the DWork vector elements

The theory is over. We know everything we need to develop our first MATLAB S-functions.

MATLAB S-functions – file source and sink blocks

We'll develop the simplest possible S-functions to enable our models to communicate with the application we described earlier: a file-source block and a file-sink block.

These S-functions will have only one port and be able to read/write a scalar real signal from/to a file. The file path will be passed as a parameter; and the files will have only one line containing the new signal value.

The sink block, called `filesink_msfun`, will receive the input and convert it to a string that will be written to the file. The file path is passed as parameter, no `DWork` vector is needed because we don't have to output a default value.

The source block, called `filesource_msfun`, will read one line from the file, attempt to convert it into a real number, and output it. When the file is not readable, the last line is empty, or an error occurs, the last valid value will be used. This means that we'll have to use one `DWork` vector, and one more parameter for the initial output.

In the following paragraphs we will walk through a detailed description of their implementation, beginning with the simpler one, the `filesink_msfun` block.

The filesink_msfun block

This block has the purpose of writing the input signal to a text file. Since the text file will be read by the external application, we can't open it once the simulation starts and close it when the simulation ends; otherwise, the application may have problems in reading it. Therefore, the file has to be opened and closed at each time step, in the `Outputs` callback.

Let's open an empty model and save it as `msfun_test.slx`.

We'll immediately place the **Level-2 MATLAB S-Function** block from the **Simulink | User-Defined Functions** blockset in our model:

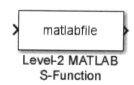

Double-clicking on the block will open the usual parameters window, where we need to replace the **S-function name** parameter with `filesink_msfun`:

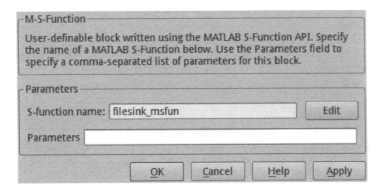

Let's click on the **Edit** button; since the `filesink_msfun.m` script file does not exist yet, Simulink will ask if we want to open the editor or locate the file. Choose the **Open editor** option to launch the MATLAB editor with an empty file, which we'll immediately save as `filesink_msfun.m`.

 A quick note to Linux users: the editor is using Emacs-like shortcuts by default (for example, *Ctrl + W/Ctrl + Y* to copy/paste). If you're not using Emacs, you may want to switch to Windows-like shortcuts (for example, *Ctrl + C/Ctrl + V* to copy/paste) by opening the **Preferences** window and navigating to **Keyboard | Shortcuts**. The first item, **Active settings**, will let you choose between Emacs or Windows behavior.

The MATLAB code

First and foremost, we need to define the S-function entry point, that is, a function with the same name as the script file itself (minus the extension), calling the mandatory `setup` callback.

```
%% S-function entry point
function filesink_msfun(block)
setup(block);
```

When Simulink updates or simulates the model, it will call `filesink_msfun`, passing as argument one `Simulink.MSFcnRunTimeBlock` object containing every data about the block itself. This will, in turn, run the `setup` callback.

The second function we must implement is the setup callback:

```
%% First required callback: setup
function setup(block)
```

The first line in this snippet of code is a comment, followed by the function definition taking the block object as argument.

Let's set the simplest block properties first: the number of parameters, input ports, and output ports.

```
block.NumDialogPrms   = 1; % Number of parameters
block.NumInputPorts   = 1; % Number of inports
block.NumOutputPorts  = 0; % Number of outports
```

In order to edit them, it's sufficient to assign the desired values to the block object's attributes. In this case, we specify that the S-function will accept only one parameter. Being a sink block, it has one input port and no output port.

We must now configure the input port:

```
% Set input port properties as inherited
block.SetPreCompInpPortInfoToDynamic;

% Override some properties: scalar real input
block.InputPort(1).Dimensions = 1;
block.InputPort(1).DatatypeID = 0; % double
block.InputPort(1).Complexity = 'Real';
block.InputPort(1).SamplingMode = 'Inherited';
block.InputPort(1).DirectFeedthrough = 1;
```

We begin by initializing the first input port properties (dimensions, datatype, complexity, and sampling mode) to be inherited from the driving block. Remember that the elements in a vector are accessed with one-based indexes.

Then we explicitly set the properties to make the input port a one-dimensional double-precision real number. The sampling mode is set as inherited from the previous block, but (unless you have the DSP System Toolbox™ product installed) the only possible value is Sample. Finally we set the DirectFeedthrough property in order to execute this block after the driving one.

We could have used the instruction block.
SetPreCompPortInfoToDefaults that would have configured the port to accept a real scalar sampled signal with a double datatype.

Since we don't have to configure any output port, we proceed by defining the sample times:

```
% Set the sample time and the offset time.
%   [0 offset]            : Continuous sample time
%   [positive_num offset] : Discrete sample time
%   [-1, 0]               : Inherited sample time
%   [-2, 0]               : Variable sample time
block.SampleTimes = [-1 0];
```

This parameter accepts a vector: the first element is the sampling time period and the second is the initial offset time (both are expressed in seconds).

The possible combinations are as follows:

- [0 Y]: For a continuous sample time with Y offset, meaning that a new sample will be acquired every time step
- [X Y]: For a discrete sampling period of X seconds with Y offset
- [-1 0]: To inherit the sample time from the driving block
- [-2 0]: To declare a variable sample time, useful only with variable-step solvers

Here we set the sample time as inherited from the driving block (-1). This block will be executed immediately after the driving one.

The next step is to define how this block should behave when the user tries to save or restore a simulation state:

```
% Specify the block simStateCompliance. The allowed values are:
%     'UnknownSimState', < The default setting; warn and assume
DefaultSimState
%     'DefaultSimState', < Same sim state as a built-in block
%     'HasNoSimState',   < No sim state
%     'CustomSimState',  < Has GetSimState and SetSimState methods
%     'DisallowSimState' < Error out when saving or restoring the model
sim state
block.SimStateCompliance = 'HasNoSimState';
```

Since this block, not having a DWork vector, has no simulation state to save or restore, we use the 'HasNoSimState' constant. Another valid option would have been 'DefaultSimState', which would end up doing nothing anyway.

To understand what a simulation state is, and when it could be useful, refer to this page in the Documentation center: **Simulink | Simulation | Run Simulation | Interactive | Save and Restore Simulation State as SimState**.

The default setting is `'UnknownSimState'`, which is equivalent to `'DefaultSimState'`, with a warning issued when the user attempts to save or restore the simulation state.

Now every block property has been defined and Simulink should be theoretically able to do a model update. But there's one information missing to complete the initialization phase. We have to register every other implemented callback at the end of the `setup` function.

Since we'll need the mandatory `Outputs` callback, we'll register it now:

```
block.RegBlockMethod('Outputs', @Outputs); % Required
```

The `RegBlockMethod` function tells Simulink that the required callback (`'Outputs'`) is implemented by another function (`@Outputs`). We could have called that function `Foo` and used `block.RegBlockMethod('Outputs', @Foo)` to register it. It's not mandatory to use the same name as the callback, but it's always better to keep things simple.

The final step is to implement the `Outputs` function's required callback:

```
%% Second required callback: Outputs
function Outputs(block)
% open the file as write-only
fid = fopen(block.DialogPrm(1).Data, 'w');
% print input port value to file
fprintf(fid, '%f', block.InputPort(1).Data);
% close the file
fclose(fid);
```

We're retrieving the value of the first parameter from the `DialogPrm` vector: it contains the filename.

The file is then opened in write mode using `fopen`, which returns the file identifier stored in `fid`.

`fprintf` will print to the file pointed by `fid` one line, that is, the number in fixed-point notation. This number is the signal we got from the first input port (accessed the same way as the parameter).

Finally, we're closing the file with `fclose`.

 File operations are found in the documentation center of the **MATLAB |
Data and File Management | Data Import and Export** section.

The script is complete. Save the `filesink_msfun.m` script and close the S-function
block properties dialog window. You'll notice that the block appearance has
changed, the output port has disappeared, and the script filename is shown without
the extension:

Let's develop the corresponding source block now.

The filesource_msfun block

The `filesource_msfun` block has the purpose of reading its output signal from a
text file, passed as parameter. Like we discussed before, the file can't be left open
since the external application will be using it too. Therefore, we have to open and
close the file at each time step.

Moreover, we have to provide a fallback value if the file isn't readable. That fallback
will be the last valid value stored in a `DWork` vector. An initial value needs to be set
via another parameter.

Repeating the same steps seen above, we add another Level-2 MATLAB S-function
to the `msfun_test.slx` model, and start developing the new script that will be called
`filesource_msfun.m`.

The MATLAB code

The S-function entry point, as we saw before, must have the same name as the file
and must execute the `setup` callback:

```
%% S-function entry point
function filesource_msfun(block)
setup(block);
```

The mandatory `setup` callback will define the block characteristics, telling Simulink there are two parameters and one scalar, real output:

```
%% First required callback: setup
function setup(block)
block.NumDialogPrms  = 2; % Number of parameters
block.NumInputPorts  = 0; % Number of inports
block.NumOutputPorts = 1; % Number of outports

% Set the default properties to all ports
block.SetPreCompPortInfoToDefaults;
```

This time we won't inherit the port characteristics from other blocks; we will just set the default options.

```
% Set the sample time and the offset time.
block.SampleTimes = [0 0];
```

The same applies to the sample time. We want the block to be run at each time step, so we're using the continuous sample time option with zero offset time.

```
% Specify the block simStateCompliance.
block.SimStateCompliance = 'DefaultSimState';
```

This block will have one `DWork` vector. By using `'DefaultSimState'`, we'll instruct Simulink to save it into the simulation state.

Since we're using a `DWork` vector, we must register the optional callbacks (`PostPropagationSetup`) to define it, set its initial value (`Start`), and perform its update (`Update`) after the outputs have been calculated:

```
block.RegBlockMethod('PostPropagationSetup',
@PostPropagationSetup);
block.RegBlockMethod('Start', @Start);
block.RegBlockMethod('Outputs', @Outputs); % Required
block.RegBlockMethod('Update', @Update);
```

Now we have to implement the callbacks, using the same order Simulink will call them with.

The first callback is the one that sets the `DWork` vector properties:

```
%% First optional callback: PostPropagationSetup
function PostPropagationSetup(block)
```

We must define how many DWork vectors we need. Since the variable that we need to store is the last valid output and there's only one output port, we need only one DWork vector:

```
block.NumDworks = 1;
block.Dwork(1).Name = 'lastValue'; % required!
block.Dwork(1).Dimensions = 1;
block.Dwork(1).DatatypeID = 0; % double
block.Dwork(1).Complexity = 'Real';
block.Dwork(1).Usage = 'DWork';
```

That vector is accessed using a one-based index. We define the vector to be one-dimensional, able to store a double datatype representing a real number. We're not interested in logging facilities, so we use the generic usage type 'DWork' (that is the default, so we could safely omit it).

The DWork vector requires the Name property to be set!

It's common practice to declare one DWork vector for each port; this way the indexes don't change and it's easy to develop and maintain the code.

The DWork vector has to be initialized before the simulation loop; this is done with the Start callback:

```
%% Second optional callback: Start
function Start(block)
block.Dwork(1).Data = block.DialogPrm(2).Data;
```

We just store the second parameter, which holds the initial output, inside the first DWork vector data.

The other required callback, Outputs, implements the logic that reads the source file:

```
%% Second required callback: Outputs
function Outputs(block)
% open file as readonly
fid = fopen(block.DialogPrm(1).Data, 'r');
% read one line
tline = fgetl(fid);
if (tline == -1) % fail
    % output last value
    block.OutputPort(1).Data = block.Dwork(1).Data;
    return
end
```

```
% convert to double
output = str2double(tline);
% check that the output is a valid number
if (isnan(output)) % fail
    % output last value
    block.OutputPort(1).Data = block.Dwork(1).Data;
    return
end
% output the read value
block.OutputPort(1).Data = output;
fclose(fid);
```

The file, whose path is the first parameter of the S-function, is opened in read-only mode with `fopen`. The `fgetl` function will attempt to read a line from the file. If the line is valid, the `str2double` function will parse it, putting the result into the `output` variable. If that variable actually contains a valid number, it is sent to the first output port. Finally the file is closed with `fclose`.

If something fails, the number stored in the first DWork vector will be sent instead, and the file is closed.

The final Update callback, called immediately after the Outputs callback, is the one that will update the DWork vector with the last output value:

```
%% Third optional callback: Update
function Update(block)
block.Dwork(1).Data = block.OutputPort(1).Data;
```

We're now done. Save the `filesource_msfun.m` script and check that the S-function block changes, having only the output port and displaying the new S-function name.

A quick test

To check that everything is working, let's add to the `msfun_test.slx` model a **Sine wave**, a **Mux**, and a **Scope**. Connect the blocks as shown in the following screenshot:

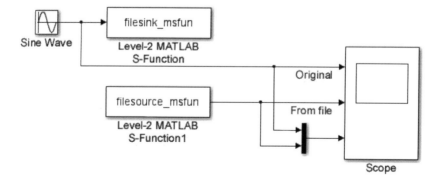

Set the **filesource_msfun** parameter to `'testfile'` `0`, and the **filesink_msfun** parameter to `'testfile'` (don't forget the single quotation marks around the filename), then set the **Fixed-Step Discrete** solver with a time step of `0.1` seconds in the Model configuration parameters window (*Ctrl* + *E*) and run the simulation.

By double-clicking on the Scope block we should see the following result:

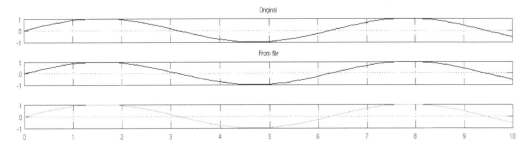

Good! The S-functions are working as expected: the **filesink_msfun** block has created the file named **testfile** in the workspace and written the **Sine wave** signal output to it. Meanwhile, the **filesource_msfun** is reading the value from the same file. A comparison of the two waves, shown in the third graph, shows that they are coincident.

If we changed the direct feedthrough setting of the **filesink_msfun** block input to 0, we would see the second wave being late by 0.1 seconds. This is because Simulink will not know that the **Sine Wave** block must be executed before the **filesink_msfun** block.

The block execution order can be viewed in the model window by selecting the **Display | Blocks | Sorted Execution Order** menu item.

We're almost ready for the real thing.

Simulink and the real world

We've got a big problem: how fast did the simulations run? Were they in sync with our real clock? The answer is no; simulation time and actual clock time are not the same. The amount of time it takes to run a simulation depends on many factors (among them are the model's complexity, the solver's step sizes, and the processor's speed). Having a very simple model (the cruise controller), powerful hardware, and a time step of 0.1 seconds, the simulation time is way ahead of the real time.

And guess what, the application we want to interface with is using the system clock.

How do we solve this problem?

Forcing Simulink to sync

We'll use the famous **Simulink Real Time Execution** S-function by Guy Rouleau, published in the MATLAB Central at the address `http://www.mathworks.com/ matlabcentral/fileexchange/21908-simulink%C2%AE-real-time-execution`.

> The MATLAB Central (`http://www.mathworks.com/ matlabcentral/`) is the main community of MATLAB and Simulink developers. You can find the latest news and updates, the blogs of many MathWorks developers, a discussion board, and the invaluable File Exchange. The File Exchange holds over 18,000 user-contributed packages, usually distributed with a permissive license like the 3-clause BSD.

The code bundle coming with this chapter already contains the `RealTimeSlower` folder with all the needed files for Windows (32 and 64 bit) and UNIX/Linux (64 bit); we only have to add that folder to our MATLAB path, as explained in *Chapter 2, Creating a Model*.

The **Simulink Library Browser** will now have a new item: the **Soft Real Time** block under the **Soft Real Time Lib** blockset. This block is the one that does the trick for us, that is, syncs Simulink to the system clock.

Preparing the cruise controller model

Let's make a copy of the cruise controller model we did in *Chapter 2, Creating a Model*, and save it to the current working folder as `cruise_control_external_msfun.slx`.

The calibration constants K_p and K_i have to be set to the values we found in *Chapter 3, Simulating a Model*. They were 0.4 and 0.002, respectively. Let's set them now:

```
Kp = 0.4;
Ki = 0.002;
```

Save the workspace as `cruise_control_external.mat`. We'll add the `load('cruise_control_external.mat')` command to the model's **PreLoadFcn** callback too, as shown in *Chapter 2, Creating a Model*.

Then we'll open the **Model configuration parameters** window (shortcut: *Ctrl + E*) and set the fixed-step solver **ode1 (Euler)**, with a **Fixed-step size** of `0.1` seconds. The simulation **Stop time** should be set to `inf`, since we want the simulation to run indefinitely until we stop it.

Finally, instead of the root-level input and output ports, we'll use the blocks we just made, along with the **Soft Real Time** block:

- The current speed input will be served by a **Level 2 MATLAB S-Function** block calling the `filesource_msfun` code, having this string as parameter `'speed.txt' 0`
- The target speed input will be served by a **Level 2 MATLAB S-Function** block calling the `filesource_msfun` code, having this string as parameter `'target.txt' 0`
- The throttle output will feed a **Level 2 MATLAB S-Function** block calling the `filesink_msfun` code, with the file `'throttle.txt'` passed as parameter
- One **Soft Real Time Lib | Soft Real Time** block will be placed into the model, right above the main block

The prepared cruise controller model should look like the following screenshot:

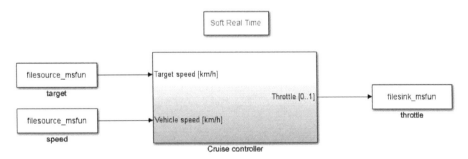

Don't forget to do a model update (shortcut: *Ctrl + D*) as a little check.

Now we're ready to have some fun!

Running the simulation on the target application

With the directions we had at the beginning of this chapter, we'll start the external application inside the same folder as the model, and set these file paths:

- The `speed.txt` file for the vehicle speed
- The `target.txt` file for the target speed
- The `throttle.txt` file for the throttle command

Before hitting the **Run** button in Simulink, hit the **Run** button in the target application first! Otherwise, our **filesource_msfun** blocks will recognize that the input files don't exist (they're created by the application as soon as its **Run** button is clicked) and throw an error. The application is less picky: the files, if they don't exist, will be automatically created.

Now we can move the **Target speed** slider, and the cruise controller will try to match it through the throttle. The simulated car will react to the throttle input, and the vehicle speed will be painted with a blue line on the application's **Speed** graph. The application will update the **Throttle** and the **Gear** graphs too.

An example is presented in the following screenshot:

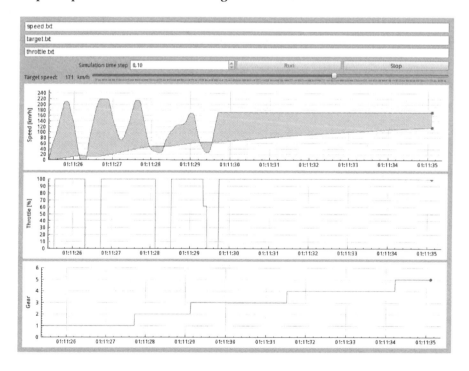

Isn't it awesome to see our Simulink cruise controller model interacting with something so different?

When we're tired of investigating how fast the car can go, measuring the 0-100 km/h time, and frantically moving the slider trying to get the Euler solver to diverge, you can stop the simulation and the application by clicking on the provided **Stop** buttons.

Want to do more? Try achieving a smoother throttle command from the cruise controller by editing K_p, K_i, and lowering the simulation step size. Be warned that file-based data exchange is highly inefficient though. (Hint: UNIX/Linux systems could use named pipes instead of standard files)

Want to do even more? The application code is really simple and is released under the GPLv2 license. You can find the most updated version at `https://github.com/sevendays/gsws-alfa147gta`. Feel free to suit the application to your needs (and let the author know)!

Going further – C MEX S-functions

Now we'll learn how to develop a custom S-function block using the C language. A basic knowledge of the C syntax is required.

The C language offers some advantages over MATLAB's scripting language:

- It is the most-used language to develop (hard) real-time systems
- It is one of the most popular languages, if not *the* most popular
- C executables offer unparalleled performance with respect to MATLAB scripts
- C S-functions can be developed without having MATLAB installed (but you'd still need the external headers and libraries)
- Legacy C code can be easily ported to S-function blocks and used in Simulink
- C++ compilers can be used, giving access to some powerful C++ frameworks like Qt

C MEX S-functions are programmed in C/C++ and built with the `mex` tool, which comes with MATLAB.

They are compiled as dynamically linked libraries on Windows platform, and as shared objects on UNIX/Linux platform, using the available compiler.

> For a list of supported compilers, go to `http://www.mathworks.com/support/compilers/current_release/`.

Setting up the mex tool

Since `mex` is only a frontend to a compiler and linker, we need to locate the available compilers in the system, and tell MATLAB which one to use.

This is easily done; just enter this command in the MATLAB main window:

```
mex -setup
```

The response is different based on the operating system in use.

UNIX-like systems (GNU/Linux in particular)

MATLAB will list the available compiler configurations, asking you to choose one: the default compiler is `gcc`, and will appear in the list if it is installed.

As soon as an option is selected, the file `mexopts.sh` containing the compiler options will be written in your home folder (usually `~/.matlab/R2013a/`).

> If you want to use C++ comments (beginning with `//`) in your C code, you can replace the string `-ansi` with `-std=c99` in your `~/.matlab/R2013a/mexopts.sh` file. Keep in mind that the next time you run `mex -setup`, your changes will be overwritten.
>
> If MATLAB complains about your gcc version being unsupported, either install the package `gcc-4.4` (or similar) if your distribution ships it, or run MATLAB inside a `chroot` with a distribution using gcc 4.4 by default, like Debian Squeeze.

Microsoft Windows systems

On Microsoft Windows systems, MATLAB will ask you for permission to automatically detect the compilers, and then it will list the available compilers, allowing you to select one.

Even if the `lcc` compiler is shipped bundled with 32-bit MATLAB for Windows, the best choice is to install the SDK provided free of charge by Microsoft, containing the `msvc` compiler. 64-bit MATLAB ships without a compiler, making it mandatory to install the SDK.

How C MEX S-functions work

Like we already learned with MATLAB S-functions, the Simulink engine requires some callbacks to be defined, and will optionally look for other callbacks.

There are four mandatory callbacks: `mdlInitializeSizes`, `mdlInitializeSampleTimes`, `mdlOutputs`, and `mdlTerminate`.

The first two belong to the initialization phase; `mdlOutputs` is called during the simulation loop and `mdlTerminate` in the cleanup phase.

The complete call graph for the initialization phase is the following one (required routines are the darker ones):

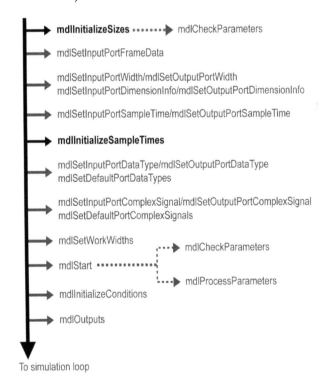

The complete call graph for the simulation and cleanup phase is the following one:

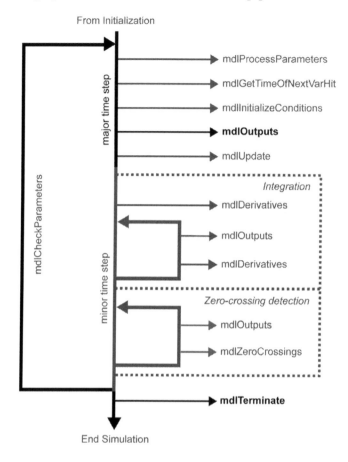

Each routine is extensively documented in the Documentation center: see **Simulink | Block Creation | Host-Specific Code | S-Function Basics | Concepts**, subsections **S-Function Callback Methods** and **S-Function SimStruct Functions**.

The required callbacks

Let's take a closer look at the required routines, and when the Simulink engine calls them.

mdlInitializeSizes

This function is used to describe the inports, outports, and characteristics of their parameters, together with the number of continuous states (integrators/derivatives), discrete states (memories), and work vectors.

It is called during the initialization phase and during a model update (it is called as soon as you configure the S-function block parameters too).

mdlInitializeSampleTimes

This function must define the sampling time period at which the S-function block operates, together with the offset time (mostly useful if the output has to be calculated after the sampling done by other blocks).

Like `mdlInitializeSizes`, it is called during the initialization phase and during a model update.

mdlOutputs

This function must implement the block's core logic, using saved states, work vectors, and input signals to calculate the block outputs.

It is called during the simulation phase, at each time step.

mdlTerminate

This function must have the cleanup logic to be executed in order to free the system resources that were allocated when the simulation started. A common usage is to close file descriptors and free the memory manually allocated with `malloc()`.

This function is called once at the end of the simulation, in the cleanup phase.

The most useful optional callbacks

These routines allow the developer to have a more fine-grained control on the S-function behavior.

Each optional routine is ignored by the Simulink engine, unless the corresponding preprocessor identifier is properly defined.

The most useful optional routines are `mdlStart`, `mdlInitializeConditions`, and `mdlUpdate`. Their main purpose, like the optional callbacks we saw while developing MATLAB S-functions, is to initialize and update block states and work vectors.

mdlStart

This function is called once, right when the simulation starts allowing you to allocate the necessary system resources. The corresponding preprocessor identifier is MDL_START.

mdlInitializeConditions

This function is called during the simulation phase, at the beginning of each time step, allowing you to reinitialize the variables stored in block states and work vectors before mdlOutputs is executed. If the S-function block is placed into an enabled subsystem, this function will be called each time the subsystem is re-enabled. The corresponding preprocessor identifier is MDL_INITIALIZE_CONDITIONS.

mdlUpdate

This function, called during the simulation phase right after the execution of mdlOutputs, serves the purpose of updating block states and work vectors.

It is called only if the block has discrete states or doesn't have direct feedthrough (otherwise there is obviously no state to update, and the Simulink engine avoids making this extra call). The corresponding preprocessor identifier is MDL_UPDATE.

> If you need to initialize persistent variables only once, use mdlStart.
>
> If, on the other hand, you need to initialize persistent variables at each simulation time step, use mdlInitializeConditions.

The DWork vector

Like its MATLAB S-function counterpart, this is the main work vector. It is able to store every datatype supported by Simulink.

Its usage is similar: the work vector characteristics, which were defined in the MATLAB S-function callback PostPropagationSetup, now have to be defined in mdlInitializeSizes.

Then, using mdlStart, initialize the values of every DWork vector and allocate the needed system resources.

Optionally, we can use mdlInitializeConditions to reinitialize the DWork vector values at the beginning of each time step.

The DWork vectors are then used by mdlOutputs to calculate the S-function block outputs and updated by mdlUpdate.

Finally, in mdlTerminate, we get the allocated system resources from the DWork vector(s) and free them up.

> Remember that DWork vectors are managed by the Simulink engine: don't attempt to free() their memory inside mdlTerminate.

There is more though. C MEX S-functions can use the so-called elementary work vectors built for the most common use cases.

The elementary work vectors

The elementary vectors that can store specific data are:

- The IWork vector can store integer data
- The RWork vector can store floating-point (real) data
- The PWork vector can store pointers to persistent data structures (such as file handlers, allocated memory, and so on)
- The Mode vector can store integer flags modifying the behavior of the S-function

Their usage is almost identical to the usage of DWork vectors described in the previous paragraphs, but with a big difference, they must be unique. This means that:

- The S-function can use only one elementary vector in mdlInitializeSizes (for example, it's not possible to have two RWork vectors in the same code, while it's possible to use the RWork vector together with the IWork vector)
- It's not possible to customize them (for example, assigning them a name)

Now that we've learned the theory behind C MEX S-functions, let's implement the same file-based source and sink blocks in C.

The filesource S-function

As we saw earlier, we need one DWork vector to store the previous block output.

Open a new file in the C editor of your preference, and call it filesource_sfun.c.

The beginning – headers and includes

The first thing to do is to define the S-function name and level, which will be used by the Simulink engine:

```
#define S_FUNCTION_NAME filesource_sfun /* mandatory */
#define S_FUNCTION_LEVEL 2              /* mandatory */
```

The S-function name is the filename without the extension. The S-function level, since Simulink release 2.2, must be always set to 2.

We may now include the required headers:

```
#include <stdio.h>    /* file manipulation functions */
#include "simstruc.h" /* mandatory */
#include "matrix.h"   /* helper functions */
```

The first header contains the system's standard I/O functions (including the file operations we'll need).

The `simstruc.h` header contains the C equivalent of MATLAB's `Simulink.MSFcnRunTimeBlock` object: a structure (`SimStruct`) representing the whole block; therefore, it's mandatory to include it.

Finally, the `matrix.h` header contains some convenient functions to operate with strings.

Block properties and memory usage – mdlInitializeSizes

We must define the block characteristics: parameters, states, ports, sample times, and work vectors.

The function begins with the following snippet of code:

```
static void mdlInitializeSizes(SimStruct *S)
{
```

Every S-function routine requires `SimStruct *S` as the first argument. This is the pointer to the Simulink block structure, maintained by the Simulink engine.

Let's define the parameters. We're going to have two parameters passed to the S-function: the first parameter is the file path, and the second is the initial output. This is accomplished by the following code:

```
/* set number of S-function parameters */
ssSetNumSFcnParams(S, 2);
if (ssGetNumSFcnParams(S) != ssGetSFcnParamsCount(S))
    return; /* Parameter mismatch will be reported by Simulink */

/* set parameters as non-tunable during simulation */
ssSetSFcnParamTunable(S, 0, SS_PRM_NOT_TUNABLE);
ssSetSFcnParamTunable(S, 1, SS_PRM_NOT_TUNABLE);
```

The function `ssSetNumSFcnParams` allows us to declare that the block accepts two parameters. The function `ssGetNumSFcnParams` will return 2, and the function `ssGetSFcnParamsCount` will return the actual number of defined parameters. If the latter isn't 2, Simulink will report an error while editing the S-function block.

Each parameter is set as `SS_PRM_NOT_TUNABLE` with the `ssSetSFcnParamTunable` function, where the second argument is the parameter index. Since we have two parameters, the function is called twice using the indexes 0 and 1. This disables the possibility of changing the parameters while the simulation is running.

Regarding the states, we don't need continuous or discrete states (we're using the `DWork` vector instead to save the previous output value). This code instructs Simulink about it:

```
ssSetNumContStates(S, 0); /* no continuous states (integrator/
derivator) */
ssSetNumDiscStates(S, 0); /* no discrete states (unit delay/
memory) */
```

Ports are easy: we only need one output port, and no input port.

```
if (!ssSetNumInputPorts(S, 0)) /* set inports number to 0 */
    return;
if (!ssSetNumOutputPorts(S, 1)) /* set outports number to 1 */
    return;
ssSetOutputPortWidth(S, 0, 1); /* set outport width (scalar) */
ssSetOutputPortDataType(S, 0, SS_DOUBLE); /* set outport type */
```

The functions `ssSetOutputPortWidth` and `ssSetOutputPortDataType` need the zero-based port index as second parameter. The former declares that the output signal is a scalar (width equal to 1), the latter that it is a real number (of datatype `double`).

We don't need a different sample time than the one used in the simulation, so we use the following code line:

```
ssSetNumSampleTimes(S, 1); /* one block-based sample time */
```

Setting the number of sample times to 1 with `ssSetNumSampleTimes` causes the block to use the global sample time only.

Finally, we need to declare a work vector that will hold the initial value and previous output. We could use the easier elementary `RWork` vector, but we're interested in learning the more generic `DWork` vector. The following snippet demonstrates its usage:

```
ssSetNumDWork(S, 1);                    /* needed vectors: 1 */
ssSetDWorkWidth(S, 0, 1);               /* the vector 0 has only 1
element */
ssSetDWorkDataType(S, 0, SS_DOUBLE);    /* and will hold a real
signal */
```

The three functions `ssSetNumDWork`, `ssSetDWorkWidth`, and `ssSetDWorkDataType` allow the Simulink engine to know how much memory should be reserved. S-functions can contain more than one `DWork` vector; their number is set with `ssSetNumDWork`. The zero-based index of the vector is then used by every other function accessing the vector itself as the second argument.

One last thing: let's put a debug statement, before the closing bracket, to ensure everything went well:

```
#ifndef NDEBUG
printf("mdlInitializeSizes called\n");
#endif
}
```

That's it; this routine now contains everything the Simulink engine needs to know in order to reserve the right amount of memory, and the debug statement will allow us to see when it is called by the Simulink engine.

Timings – mdlInitializeSampleTimes

We want to use the simulation sample time without any offset. In other words, we want this S-function block to be executed at the beginning of each time step.

The C implementation is very simple:

```
static void mdlInitializeSampleTimes(SimStruct *S)
{
    ssSetSampleTime(S, 0, CONTINUOUS_SAMPLE_TIME); /* sample always */
    ssSetOffsetTime(S, 0, 0.0);                    /* apply no offset */

    #ifndef NDEBUG
    printf("mdlInitializeSampleTimes called\n");
    #endif
}
```

The `ssSetSampleTime` and `ssSetOffsetTime` functions use the zero-based sample time index as second argument. Having declared (in `mdlInitializeSizes`) that we're using only one sample time, the index is `0`.

Since this is a source block, we define a continuous sample time. Other options are `INHERITED_SAMPLE_TIME`, `VARIABLE_SAMPLE_TIME`, and discrete sample time (any real number greater than 0).

Initial tasks – mdlStart

We'll use this optional routine to retrieve the default output parameter and store it into the DWork vector. Remember that we must define MDL_START, or Simulink will ignore the function.

The implementation is:

```
#define MDL_START  /* Change to #undef to remove function. */
#ifdef MDL_START
static void mdlStart(SimStruct *S)
{
    real_T *yPrev = NULL; /* pointer to DWork element */
    real_T yInit = 0.0;   /* tmp variable to read parameter */

    yPrev = (real_T*) ssGetDWork(S, 0);
    yInit = mxGetScalar(ssGetSFcnParam(S, 1));
    yPrev[0] = yInit;

    #ifndef NDEBUG
    printf("mdlStart: got initial output %f\n", yInit);
    #endif
}
#endif /* MDL_START */
```

The function `ssGetDWork` is used to retrieve the first `DWork` vector pointer. The index is zero based.

The function `ssGetSFcnParam` retrieves a pointer to the second parameter (the initial output), converted to a number with `mxGetScalar`. That number is saved in the first (and only) element of the `DWork` vector, accessed as an array. Remember that the number of elements was declared in `mdlInitializeSizes`.

Core logic – mdlOutputs

This routine is where the magic happens. We have to get the last line of the source file, parse the number, and output the result. If any error occurs, the recovery strategy is to output the last valid value taken from the `DWork` vector (used as a memory).

The routine definition is:

```
static void mdlOutputs(SimStruct *S, int_T tid)
{
    FILE *fd = NULL;
    char_T path[FILEPATH_LEN];
    char_T line[FILELINE_LEN];
    char_T *lineEnd;
    real_T *y = NULL;
    real_T *yPrev = NULL;
    real_T yOut;
    UNUSED_ARG(tid);

    /* get the output pointer */
    y = ssGetOutputPortRealSignal(S,0);

    /* get the previous output pointer from DWork */
    yPrev = (real_T*) ssGetDWork(S,0);

    /* get the filename for reading */
    memset(path, 0, FILEPATH_LEN);
    mxGetString(ssGetSFcnParam(S,0), path, FILEPATH_LEN);

    /* open file for reading */
    fd = fopen(path, "r");
    if(fd == NULL)
    {
        printf("Error: source file %s not readable\n", path);
        y[0] = yPrev[0];
```

```
        return;
    }

    /* get one line */
    memset(line, 0, FILELINE_LEN);
    if (fgets(line, FILELINE_LEN, fd) == NULL) /* error or empty file */
    {
        printf("Error: source file %s empty\n", path);
        y[0] = yPrev[0];
        fclose(fd);
        return;
    }

    /* convert from string to double */
    lineEnd = NULL;
    yOut = strtod(line, &lineEnd);
    if(lineEnd == line)
    {
        printf("Error: string to double conversion failed");
        y[0] = yPrev[0];
        fclose(fd);
        return;
    }

    /* if we got here everything went good */
    y[0] = yOut; /* set the output */
    fclose(fd); /* close the file */

    #ifndef NDEBUG
    printf("%s value: %f\n", path, yOut);
    #endif
}
```

We now have a second argument: tid. Blocks with more than one sample time (called multirate blocks) are run in different tasks by the Simulink engine, and tid identifies the current task being run.

Since this is not our case (we have only one sample time), we're using the UNUSED_ARG macro to avoid compiler warnings. The macro just casts the variable to void.

We've already learned how to get the DWork vectors with ssGetDWork. The ssGetOutputPortRealSignal function (accepting the zero-based port index as second argument) returns the pointer to the output port.

 Remember that ports (and signals) are arrays, even if they're scalar (their width being 1).

The first block parameter (the file name) is retrieved with ssGetSFcnParam, and converted to a string by mxGetString.

The following logic attempts to open the file, read a line from it, parse a number from the line, and output the number. If the file doesn't exist, or is empty, or there is a parsing error, the previous output is used.

Update memories – mdlUpdate

We need to save the new output into the work vector DWork:

```
#define MDL_UPDATE
#ifdef MDL_UPDATE
static void mdlUpdate(SimStruct *S, int_T tid)
{
    real_T *y = NULL;
    real_T *yPrev = NULL;
    UNUSED_ARG(tid);

    /* get the output pointer */
    y = ssGetOutputPortRealSignal(S,0);

    /* get the previous output pointer from DWork */
    yPrev = (real_T*) ssGetDWork(S,0);

    /* update the previous output */
    yPrev[0] = y[0];

    #ifndef NDEBUG
    printf("mdlUpdate: saved output %f\n", yPrev[0]);
    #endif
}
#endif /* MDL_UPDATE */
```

Being an optional function, it's necessary to define MDL_UPDATE. The rest of the code is nothing we haven't seen before; both the output signal and the work vector are mono-dimensional arrays, with only one element as specified in mdlInitializeSizes.

Cleanup – mdlTerminate

This is where we perform the cleanup, closing every system resource that has been allocated. But we don't have any.

So the C implementation is the following:

```c
static void mdlTerminate(SimStruct *S)
{
    UNUSED_ARG(S);

    #ifndef NDEBUG
    printf("mdlTerminate successfully called\n");
    #endif
}
```

This code is just an empty function that will let us know when it has been called while we're debugging. Avoid compiler warnings about unused parameters, of course.

The happy ending

One little final step has to be performed, since each S-function must have this trailer:

```c
/*=============================*
 * Required S-function trailer *
 *=============================*/
#ifdef MATLAB_MEX_FILE /* Is this file being compiled as a
 MEX-file?*/
#include "simulink.c" /* MEX-file interface mechanism */
#else
#include "cg_sfun.h" /* Code generation registration function */
#endif
```

We don't need to define MATLAB_MEX_FILE, since it is already defined by the mex tool, in order to include the necessary functions to build a MEX executable loadable by the Simulink engine.

Since automatic code generation is outside the scope of this book (and requires Simulink Coder, formerly Real-Time Workshop, which isn't cheap either), we'll ignore the cg_sfun.h header meaning.

We're done now, our first S-function is ready to be compiled.

Compiling the S-function

It's sufficient to type the following command into MATLAB's **Command Window**:

```
mex -v -g filesource_sfun.c
```

This will invoke the `mex` utility in verbose (`-v`) mode and with debugging (`-g`) enabled. This way we'll be able to read compiler messages and the `NDEBUG` preprocessor flag will be undefined.

If the compilation is successful, your folder will contain a new file:

- On 32-bit Microsoft Windows systems: `filesource_sfun.mexw32`
- On 64-bit Microsoft Windows systems: `filesource_sfun.mexw64`
- On UNIX-like systems (only 64-bit supported): `filesource_sfun.mexa64`

That file is the library Simulink will load.

Exercise – the filesink S-function

This S-function will get a real, scalar signal from its input port and write it to a file. The file name is the only S-function parameter, and the file format is the same as described earlier.

Being very similar to the filesource S-function, the source code will not be commented in detail. It's available in the code bundle provided with this book.

The reader is strongly encouraged to write and compile this S-function as an exercise following the guidelines provided below, instead of using the provided code.

We need to make a copy of the `filesource_sfun.c` file and rename it to `filesink_sfun.c`. Remember to change the mandatory definitions accordingly.

To read the input signal value, the best method is to use the `ssGetInputPortRealSignal` function. However, this requires the input signal to be set as contiguous with `ssSetInputPortRequiredContiguous`.

The sample time can be inherited from the driving block now.

An important thing that needs special attention is that by default the file writes are buffered by the operating system. You should turn off buffering by using `setbuf(fd, NULL);` right after opening the file.

The command to compile the S-function is the same as we've seen before:

```
mex -v -g filesink_sfun.c
```

The compilation will produce the `filesink_sfun` MEX file for your platform.

A quick test

Let's open the model we used to do a preliminary test on MATLAB S-functions again and save it as `sfun_test.slx`.

We only need to replace **Level 2 MATLAB S-function** blocks with **S-function** blocks. Those blocks will use the newly developed `filesource_sfun` and `filesink_sfun` as S-function names. Their parameters, as well as the model configuration, will be the same as before.

As soon as we're done editing and running a model update, a quick look at the MATLAB's **Command Window** will reveal, thanks to the debug statements we put in the code, that the `mdlInitializeSizes` routine has been called by Simulink in order to draw the new blocks' input and output ports.

Running the simulation and opening the **Scope** block should show the same results we had while testing MATLAB S-functions: both sine waves should coincide, and the MATLAB's **Command Window** will show the debug messages. Notice that `mdlStart` is called only once.

We can recompile them without the debugging macros:

```
mex -v filesource_sfun.c
mex -v filesink_sfun.c
```

Go for another ride

Let's run the application together with the cruise controller again, this time using the new S-functions.

Open the `cruise_control_external_msfun.slx` model we developed earlier, save a copy as `cruise_control_external_sfun.slx`, and replace every **Level 2 MATLAB S-function blocks** with **S-function** blocks, but keep the same parameters (except the S-function name).

Having the `cruise_control_external.mat` workspace loaded, the model configuration parameters, and the application configured as before, press the application's **Run** button, and then run the simulation.

Everything should behave as it did before:

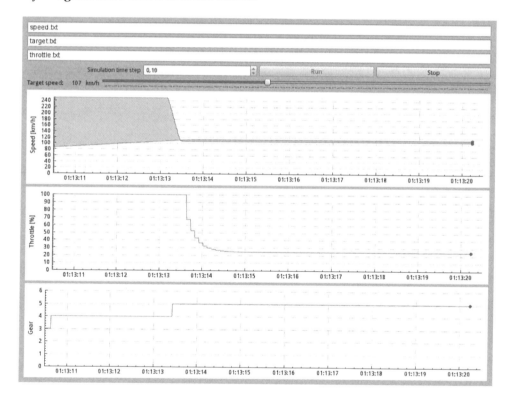

Summary

In this chapter we've learned what S-functions are and how they can be used to build custom blocks to extend the basic Simulink functionality.

We have learned which required callbacks and optional ones need to be implemented if the S-function will use work vectors to store internal states and allocate system resources.

We developed and built two simple Level 2 MATLAB S-function blocks and used them to interface the cruise controller model with an external application. Then we implemented the same block functionality in the C language, learning how to develop and build C MEX S-functions with the mex tool.

These S-functions can be used as a good starting point to develop other interfaces to communicate with virtually any application or physical device.

With the knowledge acquired in this chapter, we can greatly extend Simulink's functionality by creating new blocks or porting legacy C code to Simulink.

Index

S

T

target application
  simulation, running on 90, 91
Terminate 76
Torque to force, subsystems 40, 47

U

UNIX-like systems 92
Update 76

V

variable-step solver
  about 53
  versus fixed-step solvers 53, 54

W

Wheel to RPM, subsystems 40, 45
working folder 19
workspace
  about 19
  variables, declaring 30, 31

Thank you for buying
Getting Started with Simulink

About Packt Publishing

Packt, pronounced 'packed', published its first book "Mastering phpMyAdmin for Effective MySQL Management" in April 2004 and subsequently continued to specialize in publishing highly focused books on specific technologies and solutions.

Our books and publications share the experiences of your fellow IT professionals in adapting and customizing today's systems, applications, and frameworks. Our solution based books give you the knowledge and power to customize the software and technologies you're using to get the job done. Packt books are more specific and less general than the IT books you have seen in the past. Our unique business model allows us to bring you more focused information, giving you more of what you need to know, and less of what you don't.

Packt is a modern, yet unique publishing company, which focuses on producing quality, cutting-edge books for communities of developers, administrators, and newbies alike. For more information, please visit our website: www.packtpub.com.

About Packt Enterprise

In 2010, Packt launched two new brands, Packt Enterprise and Packt Open Source, in order to continue its focus on specialization. This book is part of the Packt Enterprise brand, home to books published on enterprise software – software created by major vendors, including (but not limited to) IBM, Microsoft and Oracle, often for use in other corporations. Its titles will offer information relevant to a range of users of this software, including administrators, developers, architects, and end users.

Writing for Packt

We welcome all inquiries from people who are interested in authoring. Book proposals should be sent to author@packtpub.com. If your book idea is still at an early stage and you would like to discuss it first before writing a formal book proposal, contact us; one of our commissioning editors will get in touch with you.

We're not just looking for published authors; if you have strong technical skills but no writing experience, our experienced editors can help you develop a writing career, or simply get some additional reward for your expertise.

MATLAB Graphics and Data Visualization Cookbook

ISBN: 978-1-849693-16-5   Paperback: 284 pages

Tell data stories with compelling graphics using this collection of data visualization recipes

1. Collection of data visualization recipes with functionalized versions of common tasks for easy integration into your data analysis workflow

2. Recipes cross-referenced with MATLAB product pages and MATLAB Central File Exchange resources for improved coverage

3. Includes hand created indices to find exactly what you need; such as application driven, or functionality driven solutions

Sage Beginner's Guide

ISBN: 978-1-849514-46-0   Paperback: 364 pages

Unlock the full potential of Sage for simplifying the automating mathematical computing

1. The best way to learn Sage which is a open source alternative to Magma, Maple, Mathematica, and MATLAB

2. Learn to use symbolic and numerical computation to simplify your work and produce publication-quality graphics

3. Numerically solve systems of equations, find roots, and analyze data from experiments or simulations

Please check **www.PacktPub.com** for information on our titles

Visual Media Processing Using MATLAB Beginner's Guide

ISBN: 978-1-849697-20-0   Paperback: 334 pages

Learn a range of techniques from enhancing and adding artistic effects to your photographs, to editing and processing your videos, all using MATLAB

1. Apply sophisticated techniques to images and videos in just a few steps

2. Learn and practice techniques for enhancing and restoring your photographs

3. Create artistic photographs using simple methods

NumPy Beginner's Guide - Second Edition

ISBN: 978-1-782166-08-5   Paperback: 310 pages

An action packed guide using real world examples of the easy to use, high performance, free open source NumPy mathematical library

1. Perform high performance calculations with clean and efficient NumPy code

2. Analyze large data sets with statistical functions

3. Execute complex linear algebra and mathematical computations

Please check **www.PacktPub.com** for information on our titles

Made in the USA
San Bernardino, CA
08 April 2018